RETIRED
& MOVED TO
FLORIDA
OLD AGE & OTHER ABSURDITIES

TOM DRYDEN

TOMDRYDEN.COM

Retired & Moved to Florida

Old Age & Other Absurdities

All Rights Reserved

Copyright © 2025 Thomas J. Dryden

OLD WAGON BOOKS

ISBN: 979-8-9885088-3-0

Cover design and interior formatting:

Mark Thomas / Coverness.com

Table of Contents

INTRODUCTION

We Baby Boomers are disappearing. One day you see us at work or walking the dog in the neighborhood; the next we've vanished like Jimmy Hoffa or Amelia Earhart. Ask about a missing Boomer and you may hear one of these responses:

A. He's dead

B. He's visiting all the national parks in his new RV

C. He's a jerk, so why do you care?

D. He retired and moved to Florida

If you are asked about me, please don't say **A** (unless you know for sure the Grim Reaper has finally punched my ticket). And definitely not **B** – I'd never be able to figure out how to drive an RV much less hook it up to a campsite. I'll be disappointed but understand if you answer **C**. I'm not everyone's cup of tea. Or vodka.

The only correct answer (for now) is **D**.

Here's the condensed story of how I ended up in the Sunshine State and how I came to write this book.

*

Back in May 1969, on the day I graduated from high school at Wentworth Military Academy, I was startled to hear the Commandant announce me as "Best English Student." (I still feel guilty I didn't confess I'm not

English, I'm American, but hey, an award is an award, and up until then I had never received recognition for anything.)

After the ceremony, my English teacher asked where I was heading for college. I told him I planned to return to Wentworth for junior college. He informed me that was a terrible idea. He said I was a good writer and suggested I enroll in the University of Missouri's Journalism School instead. I liked that idea even more when I discovered J-School students weren't required to take math or science.

Unlike most of my classmates, I wasn't interested in being a reporter—I had no desire to spend my life covering city council meetings, plane crashes, or murder trials. I wanted to write advertising, and J-School had classes for that.

After graduation, I landed a job working for the state of Missouri in Jefferson City, where I met my wife, Judy. From Jeff City, I spent two years in St. Louis writing ads for a shoe company, then moved on to a Chicago agency. In 1978, I finagled a transfer to its New York office because I knew that, "If you can make it there, you can make it anywhere." (I should copyright that line. It's catchy.)

Throughout the 1980s, I climbed the career ladder, eventually starting my own ad/promo agency in Connecticut. While continuing to create ads for stuff nobody needed, I started writing a newspaper column, *Doubting Thomas,* for my local paper in Wilton, Conn. I wrote about the absurdities of living in an upscale town filled with overachievers as well as family life, digital technology frustrations, conversations overheard in bookstores, and our idiot dachshunds.

Fast-forward to 2011: I retired. We moved to a beautiful Florida country club community with its own beach; three golf courses; tennis, pickleball and bocce courts; a kayak park; and a sailing center. Other than a yearly trip to the beach when our grandkids visit, I take advantage of none of those amenities.

People often ask, "So now that you're retired, how do you spend your time?"

Well, I walk our Jack Russell terrier two or three miles a day, work out at the gym (but never hard enough to make me sweat), play (bad) bridge, try to read a book every week, check "X" twenty times a day, and attend a weekly Happy Hour with guys from the neighborhood—all of whom have strong political opinions.

I also revived my column—this time as a blog I shared with my Facebook friends. I no longer needed to worry about deadlines or about pleasing anyone but myself. Since I was free to write more than seven hundred-fifty words, I wrote lengthier, more leisurely pieces. Most of my blog posts, some of which appear in this book, were inspired by my new life in Florida.

One day I'd write about an elderly woman at the supermarket deli counter who took a half hour ordering ham, oblivious to the hordes of customers waiting behind her. The next, about a giant iguana using our roof as his personal toilet. I wrote about a nurse at the E.R. who asked if my genitals are the ones I was born with. (Spoiler alert: I'm not sure.) And, of course, I wrote about the weirdness of getting old in a state where, miraculously, millions of residents are even older than I am.

And *Retired & Moved to Florida* isn't exclusively about my life in Florida. I had a life before I moved here and I've included a few of the more entertaining chapters from it. I've also written lots about the absurdities of life in, as Sir Paul McCartney put it so eloquently, "the ever-changing world in which we live in (sic)."

I hope these stories will make you laugh. And if they don't?

Feel free to answer **C** if anyone ever asks about me.

Way down upon the Suwannee River,
Far, far away,
There's where my heart is turning ever,
There's where the old folks stay.

All up and down the whole creation,
Sadly I roam,
Still longing for my childhood station,
And for the old folks at home.

All the world is sad and dreary
Everywhere I roam.
O dear ones, how my heart grows weary,
Far from the old folks at home.

OLD FOLKS AT HOME

Though you have probably gone through life thinking it's called *Suwannee River*, the correct name of Florida's official state song is *Old Folks at Home*. Written by Stephen Foster in 1851, it is the perfect song for a state populated by millions of retired folks who moved here to grow old around people their own age.

In many parts of the state — especially southwest Florida where I live — almost everyone seems to be a Boomer or better. Walk into a restaurant on Naples' Fifth Avenue or go to Bowman's Beach on Sanibel Island in the middle of February if you don't believe me. Florida's fastest-growing population center is The Villages, northwest of Orlando, a master planned community restricted to people fifty-five and over where you'll be surrounded by folks who remember when gas was thirty cents a gallon and nobody will be watching Tik Tok videos on their smart phones

Many old people, I freely acknowledge, don't like to be around other old folks. My sister's ex-boyfriend, a retired professor who lives in a Midwestern college town, came for a visit and kept complaining about the "old farts" he saw everywhere he went. He talked incessantly about how he stays young by living around twenty-year-old students. Those kids, whenever they see him at Starbucks, are thinking to themselves, "Why isn't he in Florida where he belongs?"

There's something nice about having neighbors who, when you mention November 22, 1963, know what happened that day.

It's nice to go to "Name That Tune" Night at the country club and to not have to identify songs by Kendrick Lamar, Taylor Swift or someone else young enough to be your grandkid. You wouldn't know them if you heard them.

It's nice to see your sixty-five-year-old friend as the bimbo secretary in the Naples Community Theater's production of *The Producers*, a role usually played by a twenty-something blonde. Nobody in the audience thinks twice about it because everyone in the cast is old, too.

It's nice to be able to go out to dinner with friends on week-nights. They're free because they, like you, don't have to go to work in the morning.

It's nice to know that, unless you are particularly obnoxious and/or have halitosis, you'll make new friends when you move here. Like you, your new friends will have arrived knowing only a handful of people who preceded them to Florida and will be eager to make new friends themselves. Unlike the friends you're leaving up north, your new friends won't prattle on and on about their children or grandchildren nor will they give a rat's ass about yours — where they went to college, how much you spent on their weddings, what they do for a living, or how many spawns they produced. That will be a welcome change, especially if the adult offspring you left behind are stupid losers you are embarrassed to talk about.

That said, there are drawbacks to being surrounded by old folks.

Go to Happy Hour or dinner with friends and you'll spend the first half of it discussing the latest ailments and/or treatments at least one of them is enduring.

You'll receive emails on a regular basis from your Homeowners'

Association or country club announcing, "So and So passed away Tuesday, October 14. He is survived by his wife of forty-nine years, blah, blah." The constant death notices are reminders you already have one foot in the crematorium yourself.

You will run across people whose memories, to put it charitably, aren't as sharp as they once were.

I play bridge with a group of people my age and older. I'm astonished so many of them are able to discuss in forensic detail plays they wish they had made a month ago. *"I should have played my Jack instead of my nine when Bill played his eight because Jane had the ten and took the trick."* But none of them (or me, for that matter) can remember who dealt the hand they're currently playing.

My wife and I enjoy Trivia Night at our community center. One night we sat at a table with a distinguished-looking couple in their late seventies or early eighties. The wife, we noticed, didn't contribute a single answer; she just sat there with a blank look. After the game, she congratulated my wife for knowing the answer that ultimately made our table the winner of that night's jackpot. (*"What did John Travolta and Kelly Preston name their daughter?" Ella Blue, of course.*) "I wish I could remember things like that," the woman said wistfully. "I even went to a seminar the other day to see what I could do about improving my memory."

"What did you learn?" my wife asked. "I don't remember," she answered with a shrug. Then she started laughing. And everyone at our table laughed along with her.

If you are going to be losing your memory, eyesight, coordination, hearing and/or your hair, there's something to be said about losing it around people in the same boat who can laugh, or at least empathize about it, with you.

THE COLONOSCOPY

10:45 a.m.

TD *(to hospital front desk receptionist)*: I have an appointment for a colonoscopy. I'm supposed to be here an hour early. Where do I go?

Receptionist: Can you tell me your name?

TD: Thomas Dryden.

Receptionist: Middle initial?

TD: J for Joseph.

Receptionist: Date of birth?

TD: November 17, 1951.

Receptionist: Take the elevator to the third floor and turn left. The GI lab is the second door on the right.

TD: Thank you.

10:48 a.m.

TD *(to GI lab receptionist)*: My name is Tom Dryden. I have an appointment for a colonoscopy.

Receptionist: Your full name?

TD: Thomas J. Dryden

Receptionist: Your date of birth?

TD: November 17, 1951.

Receptionist: OK, somebody will be with you in a minute.

11 a.m.

Admitting Clerk: Thomas?

TD: Right here!

Admitting Clerk: Come with me. Have a seat. What is your full name?

TD: You called my name. You know it.

Admitting Clerk: I have to ask. It's the law.

TD: Thomas J. Dryden.

Admitting Clerk: What's your date of birth?

TD: November 17, 1951.

Admitting Clerk: Do you know why you're here?

TD: Of course. Do you think I'm here for the sport of it?

Admitting Clerk: Okay then, why?

TD: I'm having a colonoscopy.

Admitting Clerk: I see we have your insurance information. Go back to the lobby and a nurse will be calling you shortly.

11:16 a.m.

Nurse: Thomas?

TD: Yes?

Nurse: Follow me please. Here's the room where you'll be changing into a gown and waiting to go into the procedure room. Can you tell me your name?

TD: Why do you people keep asking me this? It's not instilling much confidence you know what you're doing.

Nurse: It's a requirement.

TD: Thomas J. Dryden

Nurse: Birthdate?

TD: November 17, 1951.

Nurse: And what procedure are you having done today?

TD: A lobotomy.

Nurse: That's not what it says here.

TD: Colonoscopy.

Nurse: Here's a gown and a plastic bag. Put the gown on, leave it loosely tied in back, and place any valuables — your wallet, Kindle, glasses, cell phone, etc. — in the bag.

TD: All right.

11:30 a.m.

Anesthesiologist *(to me as I'm lying on gurney)*: Hello, I'm Dr. Payne. (I am not making this up. That was his name.) I'll be administering your anesthesia today. Can you tell me your name?

TD: On one condition.

Anesthesiologist: What's that?

TD: That you won't ask my date of birth.

Anesthesiologist: I have to.

TD: OK, Thomas J. Dryden, November 17, 1951. Please knock me out now so I won't have to answer that again.

Anesthesiologist: I can't do that until we're in the procedure room. An aide will be coming to take you there in a few minutes.

11:42 a.m.

Aide: Hi, I'm Michael. I'll be wheeling you into the procedure room. Are you ready?

TD: Ted Bundy. January 24, 1989.

Aide: I beg your pardon?

TD: Never mind.

11:44 a.m.

Gastroenterologist: Hi Tom, how are you today? Are you ready to get this over with?

TD: I didn't think there could be anything more annoying than drinking two jugs of that lime-green laxative stuff and spending the night on the toilet, but I was wrong. Did you know that …

Gastroenterologist: Can you tell me your full name and date of birth?

TD: I had an appointment with you three days ago! Don't you remember me?

Gastroenterologist: It's policy.

TD: My God, please, please put me out now. I can't do this anymore.

Gastroenterologist: Do what?

TD: Tell you my name and date of birth one more time.

Gastroenterologist: I have to ask.

TD: Thomas Joseph Dryden. November 17, 1951.

Gastroenterologist: Can you tell me why you're here?

TD: I'm having a C-section — twins, but it might be triplets, I think I felt an extra heartbeat today.

Gastroenterologist: There's no reason to yell.

TD: I'm sorry, but this is fucking insane.

Gastroenterologist: Well, I'd like to remind you I'm holding a five-foot hose I'm about to shove up your ass. I can be gentle but if you won't cooperate, I might not be.

TD: Because I'm having a colonoscopy. I'm sick and tired of having to answer the same questions over and over and over. Look what the blood pressure monitor says. I'm about to … aaaaaahhhhhhhhhhh (*anesthesia kicks in*).

12:15 p.m.

Nurse: Hi, Mr. Dryden. It's over, you're in the recovery room. The doctor will be here to go over the results in a few minutes.

TD: Huh? Ugg … ga … ga…

Nurse: Can you tell me your name and date of birth?

THE LIQUIDATION LADIES

Our Connecticut house was a two-story frame colonial with front and back staircases, three fireplaces and — my favorite room, I designed it myself — a wood-paneled library with shelves of books. It was surrounded by a white picket fence and the two-acre property was delineated from its neighbors by stone walls my wife and I liked to think had been built by pilgrims — the town was settled in 1634.

Our Florida house is a vaguely Mediterranean contemporary single story. It has a tile roof, twelve-foot ceilings, and a wall of sliders leading to the lanai and pool. The property is planted with palm trees, palmettos, bougainvillea and hibiscus. The first home in our development was built in the early nineties and there are still two high-rises under construction.

Hardly anything in the Connecticut house was appropriate for the Florida house. So when we signed a contract to sell our northern home, we had four weeks to decide what to do with its contents, the detritus of the life we were leaving behind.

We could, of course, have packed everything up and moved it with us. But we didn't have room for it. We had purchased our Florida house six years earlier and my wife had furnished, decorated and equipped it for our new child-free tropical lifestyle.

So we called our grown children, who drove up from D.C. The eldest had recently gotten married and he and his wife had a new condo. We assumed they would be glad to have lots of our stuff — especially the good pieces — to fill it. But they only wanted a box of picture frames. As all Millennials apparently do, they want the "Pottery Barn look." Our youngest, who was just starting his career and living in a tiny rental, took some plates, flatware, pots and pans, a coffee table, a lamp, a framed print, and sports trophies.

We went through the house to choose things we couldn't bear to part with — the baby grand, an antique bookcase from my mother, a marble-topped table from my wife's grandparents, two sets of china, a couple of hundred books, and the cremated remains of five dogs. We hired Mayflower to move those.

We then considered options for disposing of the remainder of our stuff. We could:

Option A: Sell it on Craigslist or Facebook marketplace.

Option B: Hold the mother of all tag sales.

Option C: Pay someone to take it to a consignment shop.

Option D: Donate everything to charity. This option was particularly appealing because charities often give donors blank receipts to list what they donate, enabling them to deduct the total value of the items from their taxes, such as:

- *Tommy Roe's Greatest Hits* album, $150
- Avocado green fondue pot, $100
- Electric windshield ice scraper, $75
- Dachshund lamp, $250
- Etc.

We chose none of those options.

To our eternal regret, we called "The Liquidation Ladies," Shirley and Audrey, specialists in organizing and running sales for homeowners looking to sell the contents of their houses. Their ads promoting upcoming sales had been running in our local newspaper for years.

The Ladies impressed me by arriving in a late model BMW 7-series sedan. My wife was impressed by their clothes, shoes, handbags and jewelry. Both were around our age — maybe a few years older. Shirley told us she had been an interior decorator serving mostly Greenwich (rich) clients but had sold her business. Audrey said she had been in investment banking. Ten years ago they met at a fundraiser, discovered they both enjoyed helping people, and decided to go into business together. They couldn't begin to count how many sales they had run on behalf of clients our age who, like us, were moving to Florida.

Shirley and Audrey said they loved everything in the house. They complimented my wife's taste in furniture, china, glassware, lamps, appliances, rugs and clothes. They even loved my high school saxophone that had lost its gold plating and pads. They said everything in the house would sell for top dollar and they would split the take with us fifty/fifty.

They assured us there was nothing for us to do; they would handle everything. Shirley suggested we consider taking a mini-vacation the weekend of the two-day sale, which was scheduled to end at 5 p.m. on Sunday before we were to sign the papers transferring ownership of our house the next afternoon. She said some of their clients got emotional when they saw sentimental items being taken away by new owners and she didn't want us to feel sad.

The Ladies promised to return the Monday before the sale and said they would most likely be working in our house for four, maybe five, days to prepare everything for the hordes of loyal followers they said showed up for sales run by the Liquidation Ladies.

That was the last we heard from them until noon the day before the sale was to begin. They didn't answer their phones, or reply to our emails and texts.

We would have assumed they had skipped town if we hadn't seen the ad in our local newspaper announcing our sale. Needless to say we were beside ourselves when the Ladies, along with their toothless crackhead helper, Germaine, finally showed up. When I asked where the hell they had been, Shirley, who was wearing a neck brace, said she had been in the hospital recovering from back surgery. Audrey said she had been in, of all places, Florida, planning and attending her granddaughter's wedding.

From noon until well after midnight, Audrey and Germaine set up clothes racks in the living room; emptied kitchen cabinets, drawers and shelves; arranged dishes, glassware, pots, pans and knick-knacks on tables; and placed price tags on everything. Shirley, who said she was unable to lift anything due to her surgery, reclined on a chaise lounge on the deck, chain-smoking and talking on her phone.

Germaine moved furniture from the second floor to the first, gouging the freshly-painted walls and scratching the hardwood floors that had been refinished to make the house more appealing to potential buyers.

The Ladies explained that anything that failed to sell the first day would be marked down fifty percent the second day. That would assure the house was delivered empty to its new owners. They even reminded us to rent a hotel room for our final night in Connecticut because our poster bed would, of course, have been sold, along with all the other beds.

But traffic the next day was light. Those who did stop in clearly didn't want what we were selling; nothing was from Pottery Barn. At one point I stopped Germaine, who was carrying a pipe wrench as he was about to go to the basement, and asked what he was doing. He said he needed the wrench to disconnect the Culligan Water System one of the Ladies had sold for two-hundred dollars. I said no, it conveyed with the house.

By the end of the day the Liquidation Ladies had sold a grand total of two sofas, six lamps, a wingback chair, three end tables, two coffee tables, a mattress, two chests of drawers, three rugs, an electric quesadilla maker, a cast iron patio set, a pair of snow tires, a china cabinet, the saxophone, and seven or eight boxes of books.

It rained the second and final day so traffic was even lighter. Mid-morning, Shirley and Audrey started marking lamps for which we had paid five hundred dollars down to ten dollars, upholstered chairs to five dollars, Waterford goblets to fifty cents apiece, and inviting customers to help themselves to books, records and clothes. At 5 p.m. when the "Another Fabulous Liquidation Ladies Sale!" sign was removed from the front yard, the vast majority of our possessions remained unsold, less than twenty-four hours before the house had to be broom-clean for its new owners.

The Ladies and Germaine drove away, promising to return in an hour with a Ryder truck to take the most valuable pieces that hadn't sold to local consignment shops and auction houses. That way, we would at least get something for them. Everything else would be delivered to Goodwill, so we could deduct the value from our taxes. They said they would bring an itemized list the next morning, so we would know where our things had been taken, and handed us a check for three thousand seven hundred twelve dollars — our half of the proceeds from the sale. The saxophone had sold for three hundred dollars, the highest price of the day. That was a hundred dollars more than the pristine mahogany Baker dining room set — an oval table with two extensions, eight matching chairs, and sideboard — Shirley's niece from Bridgeport had purchased and taken away while my wife and I were at Subway buying lunch for the Ladies and Germaine who had forgotten to bring theirs.

Just before 10 p.m., Audrey and Germaine showed up with the truck. They said they had reserved one from the Norwalk office but it was gone when they arrived, so they had to go all the way to Queens for it. When Germaine backed it up the driveway, he took out the picket fence. Audrey said Shirley, poor thing, was worn out and unable to help — she shouldn't have worked the sale because she hadn't recovered from her back surgery, but she had wanted to be there for us because she liked us, we were good people.

For the next five hours Audrey, Germaine and I carried out our remaining possessions — an antique Swedish hutch; an almost new leather sectional; four beds; chests of drawers; dressers; box after box of crystal, china and flatware; appliances; sports equipment; clothes; throw pillows; vases; TVs; pots; pans; end tables; coffee tables; a kitchen table with matching chairs; occasional tables; bicycles; tools; a silver tea service; computer equipment; club chairs; bar stools; ottomans; ladders; box after box after box of books; fireplace tools; CDs and record albums; knick-knacks; paddy whacks; clothes; bed linens; table linens; and much, much, much more — and threw them into the back of the Ryder truck. You could hear the crystal wine glasses we had purchased one stem at a time in the early years of our marriage being smashed to smithereens under the rubble. They drove away shortly before 3 a.m. That was the last we heard from the Ladies.

Needless to say, we never received the promised accounting of what they had taken or where they had taken it. I suspect they dropped everything off at a resale shop in which they were silent partners, giddy at having suckered another gullible couple into hiring them to liquidate belongings they had accumulated thoughtfully and carefully over their years together.

In retrospect, it would have caused us less grief and angst to toss thirty-seven years' worth of possessions into a pile, douse it with gasoline, and throw a match on it. I wish we had done that. And I wish we had tossed Shirley, Audrey and Germaine in, too.

Dryden's rules for the Florida-bound

Rule 1: Do not, under any circumstances, hold an estate sale.

Rule 2: If you disregard Rule 2, do not hire ladies named Shirley or Audrey to run it.

Rule 3: Do not allow your wife to become so emotional as you leave the home in which you raised your family that, three hours after you are headed south through a neighboring state, you realize you left your dachshunds in the basement.

THE WIZARD AUXVASSE

Missouri has many small towns with peculiar names. Peculiar, for instance. Not to mention Blue Eye, Tightwad, Useful, Cooter, and Climax Springs. Strange names to be sure, but at least they are pronounceable.

The name of my hometown, Auxvasse, is damn near impossible for anyone but a native to pronounce.

Outsiders try to pronounce it phonetically — *Ox Vossy*. Or, if they know a little French, they'll say *Oh Vwah,* which certainly sounds classy. Both are way off base.

Google Gemini AI says it should be pronounced *Awe Vaz*. ChatGPT, another AI, says the first syllable is pronounced "oh" and the second "vass" which rhymes with "mass." They may have access to all the knowledge mankind has accumulated over the years, but they are wrong, too.

When asked how one pronounces the Missouri town spelled a-u-x-v-a-s-s-e, Alexa, Amazon's virtual assistant, is baffled. "Hmm," she replies. "I'm not sure how to help you with that." Apple's Siri can't pronounce it either.

For years I explained to people who asked, "It's pronounced like the last two words in the title of the movie about Dorothy and Toto, *The Wizard Blank Blank.* Say it out aloud and fill in the missing words, *The Wizard Blank Blank.*"

"I get it!" they shout. "The Wizard *OF OZ!*" But that's not one hundred percent right either.

To pronounce it as we natives do, say *gauze*. Then drop the g, put "of" in front of it, and *voila*, you've got it: *Of auze.*

The town was founded in 1871 as Clinton City. A few months later someone figured out the reason nobody had received any mail was because there was already a Missouri town named Clinton to which all the mail intended for Clinton City was being delivered. The Postal Service insisted on a new name.

The town's founders, who clearly weren't all that swift when it came to picking names in the first place, decided to name the town after a nearby creek. Legend has it the creek was named by French settlers whose wagons had become stuck in its muck. The Frenchies dubbed the creek *Riviere Aux Vases* which supposedly means "river with miry places." A friend from France tells me Auxvasse actually means "to the bottle" which may explain why the town's tavern is one of the few long-time businesses that has survived.

I like to amuse myself on long trips by challenging my car's navigation system to perform complicated tasks. I will ask it, for example, to route me to Anchorage, Alaska. Within seconds, it calculates the route and an AI-generated voice that sounds remarkably like Rosie, the Jetsons' robot, tells me every road I need to take and every turn I need to make.

But no matter how many times I ask, it can't figure out how to get me to Auxvasse because it, like everyone else, can't comprehend what I am saying.

"Do you want to access navigation?" asks the digital voice.

"Yes," I reply.

"OK, what state?"

"Missouri."

"Mizz-her-ee," the voice confirms. "What city?"

"Of Oz," I say.

The screen then displays a list of five possibilities. The choices are different every time but almost always include Augusta, Oakwood or Bogard. Not once has it given me the option of going where I told it to take me.

If I had to rely on my car's navigation system I would never be able to find my way home again. And as people continue to depend increasingly on technology rather than printed maps to tell them how to get from point A to point B, Auxvasse may someday prove impossible for anyone to find unless, of course, the good people of that town change the name again to something a computer can understand.

"Clinton City" contained the name of a future president and was easy to pronounce. A computer would have no trouble understanding that. So maybe the town can be renamed for another president. Bidenville. Trump Town. Just as long it's comprehensible.

It was such a hassle having to explain the inevitable pronunciation question that I stopped telling people I'm from Auxvasse. It was too complicated. And it's not like anyone ever asked, "Do you know so-and-so from there?" I spent most of my life in the New York area. New Yorkers have never met anyone from Missouri, much less from Auxvasse.

So now, when people ask where I'm from, I lie and say I'm from the town that is nearest to Auxvasse. It's the town I was born in because it, unlike Auxvasse, had a hospital.

"I'm from Mexico," I tell them.

"Wow," they say. "Never met a Mexican with blue eyes."

It's easier to leave it at that.

OSCAR ACCEPTANCE SPEECH

Oh my God, thank you! You like me, you really do! There are so, so many people I want to mention. Excuse me, I'm shaking. I never dreamed I'd be standing here.

(Writer name), from the first page, I knew you had written the perfect script.

(Director name), thank you for giving me the honor of bringing (character name) to life.

My co-stars (actor name and actor name) — this belongs as much to you as it does to me.

My beloved (partner), as valuable as this statue is, you know that waking up next to you every morning is the prize I value most.

The only thing that could possibly make me happier tonight is if that orange orangutan fascist in the White House were to be strung up from the top of the Washington Monument — not just him but all the lying thieves in his cabinet and the ignorant racist white trash who voted for him. Every time I see his fat face swollen with the festering puss of misogyny, xenophobia, pedophilia and homophobia, I want to puke. All of you watching at home know he is nothing but Putin's puppet and that if he were to get his way and all the immigrants, gays and transgenders were exterminated, there wouldn't be anyone left in this town to create the movies that encourage, uplift, inspire and remind us of our humanity.

I hope all of you who share my fear that the America in which our children are growing up makes Nazi Germany look like *Mr. Rogers' Neighborhood* will remember that, and will never, ever forget the most important thing of all — that love trumps hate.

Thank you all so much. I love you!

DOG CRAZY

A black Mercedes S-class sedan with Ontario plates was parked in front of the entrance to the kennel and spa when I arrived this morning to pick up Rupert and Russell, our dogs who had been boarded overnight.

Standing in front of the check-in desk, cradling a fluffy white dog with a pink bow atop its head, was the owner of this magnificent feat of German engineering, a woman who looked remarkably like Sarah Palin, down to the rimless glasses. She — the woman, not the dog — was wearing a tennis outfit, diamond earrings in a cross-cross pattern and, on her left hand, a solitaire roughly the size of a robin's egg. A Nordstrom's shopping bag was atop the check-in counter.

"Here's her water dish," she said, reaching into the bag and handing the dish to the clerk, a frizzy-haired woman about my age. The bowl was engraved with the dog's name, Evelyn.

"And here's her water," she said, removing a bottle of Nestle Pure Life. "Please make sure you don't give her tap water by mistake. This is all she drinks and she needs to stay hydrated, especially now that we're back in Florida."

"OK," the attendant said, nodding her head.

"Here's her food dish and food," Evelyn's mother announced, pulling from the bag a tiny ceramic bowl and two plastic containers. "She gets the chicken for lunch — she eats around noon, just before she goes down for her nap — and the turkey snack around 4:30. You'll need to keep it refrigerated, of course."

"Of course," the attendant replied.

"Do you have a microwave?"

"Yes, in the break room,"

"Well, she won't eat cold food so you'll need to nuke it, but just for three or four seconds. It needs to be at room temperature or even a tiny bit warmer, but not hot. Please, *please* make sure the bowl isn't hot to the touch before you give it to her."

"All right," the attendant said.

"And she gets one of these vitamins with her lunch," the woman said, handing the attendant a bottle. "You'll have to open the capsule and mix it in with her food."

"One vitamin at lunch, break open capsule and mix with food," the attendant repeated, typing into her computer.

"She was just groomed yesterday," the woman said. "I tried to remove the bow but it's clipped on so tight with a rubber band, and I'm afraid she'll lose it. It's adorable, don't you think?"

"If she loses it, we'll put another one on her," the attendant said, ignoring the question. "We're a full-service grooming salon."

"If you have to do that, make sure it's pink. Evie likes pink, don't you?" she asked the dog. I half expected Evelyn to reply.

"Oh my God!" the woman shrieked, as if she had been goosed. "I forgot her bed! How could I have done that? I'll run out to the car and get it." She turned and, clutching Evelyn like a running back clutches a football, exited.

She returned a moment later with a tiny doggy bed in a leopard skin print. "Here you go," she said, handing it to the attendant. "What time is nap time?"

"From one to two," the attendant told her.

"That's perfect — exactly her schedule, isn't it Evie?" the woman asked Evelyn, who yawned.

Is there anything else?" the attendant asked solicitously.

"I can't think of it but if I remember something I'll call you," the woman replied, kissing Evelyn repeatedly, as if she were going off to war. She lifted the dog over the counter and placed her in the attendant's arms.

The attendant rang a bell and spoke into a loudspeaker. "We have a check-in."

A sullen-looking girl appeared from the back room and took the dog from the clerk.

"Isn't she the sweetest thing you ever saw?" the woman asked, watching Evelyn disappear into the back room from which, when the door opened, the already shrill sound of dogs barking became almost deafening, but she wasn't addressing the attendant or me. She was talking to herself, as if she were watching Jesus walk on water.

"What time are you picking her up this afternoon?" the attendant asked.

"I'm going to try to be here by five-thirty but it may be closer to six if there's traffic."

"OK, we'll see you then."

The woman turned, went out the door, and got into her car.

"You're here for Rupert and Russell, right?" the attendant asked me.

"Yes," I said. "And I hope you'll remember in the future that they prefer Fiji Water, not plain old Nestle. That was absolutely amazing."

"I could write a book about these people," she replied with a weary smile.

"I bet you could," I told her, as our dogs led the girl out of the back room, straining their leashes to get out of that place so they could return to their lives and try to forget that, for twenty-four hours, someone may have actually considered them to be — horrors — animals.

"What took you so long?" my wife asked when I returned with the dogs who, having no idea whether they had been boarded for one day or one year, started yelping with joy when they saw her, just like the dogs in those YouTube videos when their soldier masters return from overseas.

"I thought nobody could possibly be crazier about their dogs than we are," I told her between yelps. "But I was wrong."

CALLING THE AUDIOLOGIST

Receptionist: Thank you for calling Palmetto Coast Audiology Associates. How can I help you?

TD: I'd like to schedule an appointment.

Receptionist: Are you a new patient?

TD: Yes.

Receptionist: What's your first name?

TD: Thomas.

Receptionist: And your last name?

TD: Dryden. That's D-R-Y-D-E-N.

Receptionist: You said Bryban, right?

TD: No, not bry, *dry*. As in, "The desert is dry." D as in Delta, R as in Roy and Y as in Yellow.

Receptionist: OK, got it. Dryban.

TD: *No!* Not ban, *den*. A place where lions live. That's D as in Delta, E as in Edward and N as in Nancy.

Receptionist: OK, Mr. Den. Got it.

TD: No, no, no! My last name is *Dry-den*, D-R-Y-D-E-N. Ever heard of the Canadian hockey goalie Ken Dryden?

Receptionist: No.

TD: How about the English poet John Dryden?

Receptionist: Never heard of him either but I got it — Thomas D-R-Y-D-E-N. Let me see when I can get you in.

TD: No rush, I have been putting this off for years. I can wait.

Receptionist: There's an appointment available July eighth at noon at our Bonita office. Would that be convenient?

TD: Wow, yes. That's fast service! Thank you.

Receptionist: OK, let me get some more information while I have you on the phone. What's your date of birth?

TD: November 17, 1951.

Receptionist: September did you say?

TD: I said November.

Receptionist: You don't have to raise your voice.

TD: I'm sorry but this is frustrating. I'll admit I can't hear squat — that's why I'm calling — but there's nothing wrong with my speech. Do you wear the hearing aids your company sells? If so, maybe I should go elsewhere.

Receptionist: No, my hearing is fine. What day and year did you say?

TD: November seventeenth nineteen fifty-one.

Receptionist (talking to herself as she is typing into her computer): November seventh, nineteen fifty-one.

TD: Not the seventh, November seven-*teenth!* Is *Candid Camera* recording this conversation? Is this some sort of joke? If so, it's a cruel one, making fun of deaf people.

Receptionist: What's *Candid Camera*?

TD: Never mind.

Receptionist: OK Mr. Dryden, we will see you tomorrow, July eighth at 1 pm.

TD: Uh, wait a minute, I'm looking at my calendar and today's the sixth. Tomorrow is the seventh, not the eighth. Is my appointment tomorrow the seventh or Wednesday the eighth?

Receptionist: The eighth.

TD: Thanks for clarifying that.

Receptionist: That's what I just said.

TD: Yes, but you said tomorrow and the eighth is Wednesday.

Receptionist: OK, we'll see you in our Bonita office tomorrow July (unintelligible) at noon. Thanks for calling.

WINNER WINNER CHICKEN DINNER

When: Last night between 7 and 7:30.

Where: Three fast food franchise restaurants along U.S. 41 in Southwest Florida.

Who: Myself and employees of KFC, Popeye's and Church's Chicken respectively.

7:02 p.m., KFC

Employee: What would you like?

TD: I want a two-piece meal with potatoes and gravy and I'd like one of the pieces to be a breast.

Employee: We're out of chicken.

TD: What do you mean?

Employee: We ran out.

TD: Let me get this straight, you're out of chicken? Isn't this a Kentucky Fried Chicken?

Employee: No, this a KFC. And we're also a Taco Bell. How about a chicken taco or burrito?

TD: No, I'm craving fried chicken.

7:14 p.m., Popeye's

Employee: Can I take your order?

TD: I want a two-piece meal with a side of mashed potatoes and gravy and I'd like one of the pieces to be a breast.

Employee: We're out of chicken parts, we only have chicken tenders.

TD: You're kidding, right?

Employee: They're really good. No bones. I just ate two on my break.

TD: I can't believe this. No thanks.

7:30 p.m., Church's

Employee: Can I help you?

TD: I want a two-piece meal with a side of mashed potatoes and gravy. I'd like one of those pieces to be a breast.

Employee: Original or spicy?

TD: You have chicken? Great! I'll take original.

Employee: Do you want our two-piece deal? It comes with a biscuit and a medium drink.

TD: Absolutely!

Employee: OK, that'll be nine dollars eighty-nine cents.
(Two minutes later I am handed my order on a tray. I fill my soft drink cup from the dispenser, sit at a table in the dining area where I am the only customer, and realize I need a fork. I get up and go to the counter where the condiments, napkins and plastic utensils are kept. The utensil bins are empty except for knives.)

TD *(to employee)***:** There aren't any forks on the counter. Can I have one?

Employee: We're out of forks.

TD: OK then, a spoon.

Employee: We're out of those too.

TD: How do you expect me to eat my mashed potatoes?

Employee: Would you like Cajun fries instead?

TD: No.

Employee: How about some mac and cheese, coleslaw or rice and beans?

TD: How would I eat those? With a knife?

Employee: I'm sorry.

TD: How long have you been out of forks and spoons?

Employee: Ever since I came on at 5. Well, now that I think about it, we were out of them yesterday, too.

TD: Hasn't anyone else complained but me?

Employee: No, you're the first. Everyone else goes through the drive-through.

LUNCH WITH
TOM AND WILL

Hostess: Is this table okay?

Tom and Will: It's fine, thanks.

Tom *(addressing Will):* So, you're looking fit. How come you're wearing a suit? I thought you were coming from the golf course?

Will: Going to a memorial service.

Tom: Who died?

Will: The president of our community association. He was trimming a palm by his pool and, kaboom, a massive heart attack – dead before he hit the ground.

Tom: Seems like you're always going to funerals or memorial services. Whose was it last time we were supposed to have lunch and you had to cancel?

Will: My cousin in Boca.

Tom: Oh yeah, I remember.

Will: Third service this month. They're dropping like flies I tell you.

Tom: What's with all those bandages on your face?

Will: Had a dermatologist appointment this morning to have some growths removed. He's almost sure they're squamous. If that's the case I'll have to have Moh's surgery.

Tom: Yikes. Are you fully recovered after your ...your ... what was that procedure you were about to have last time I saw you?

Will: Which one? I had three – an MRI, a CAT scan and a cystoscopy.

Tom: Uh, the last one. What's that about?

Will: They shove a camera up your dick and take pictures of your bladder.

Tom: Holy shit! How big is the camera?

Will: I dunno. I was knocked out. Didn't see it.

Tom: I've never heard of such a thing. It's making me nauseous to even ...

Will: I pissed blood for two days after.

Tom: I'm sorry I asked. Let's change the ...

Will: The urologist says everything looks fine.

Tom: Well that's good.

Will: Next week I'm having a prostate biopsy.

Tom: Jeez.

Will: They take twelve pieces of tissue.

Tom: Why are you having that?

Will: My PSA's borderline high. Do you know yours?

Tom: Yes. It's fine. So, how's Marilyn?

Will: I'm taking her to the hospital tomorrow at 7 a.m. for surgery.

Tom: What's wrong?

Will: Nothing life-threatening. They're repairing her rotator cuff. She tore it playing tennis.

Tom: This isn't your month, is it?

Will: We oughta order, the service starts at 2. What are you going to have?

Tom: Same thing I always get, the mahi-mahi sandwich.

Will: Uh, I don't think there's anything I can eat on this menu.

Tom: What do you mean? We've eaten here a dozen times. The mahi-mahi sandwich is good. Tell them to grill it, that's healthy.

Will: My doctor told me not to eat fish. He ran a blood test. It showed I have toxic levels of mercury in my system. He says it's because we eat too much fish.

Tom: Well, they make a great burger here.

Will: My cholesterol's too high. It's off the charts even with the statins I take.

Tom (*reading from menu*): Here you go: "Two scoops of cottage cheese surrounded by seasonal fruit." Surely you can eat that.

Will: Nope. Just found out I'm lactose-intolerant.

Tom: Well, the rolls here are good. You can eat some of those while I eat my sandwich.

Will: Do you know if they have any that are gluten-free?

Tom: I wouldn't know. How are those nice neighbors we met at your house last month? We really hit it off with them. We oughta all go out together some night.

Will: Andy and Mary Beth?

Tom: Yeah.

Will: He's dead.

Tom: What? He couldn't have been much over — I'd have to guess — sixty at the most. He looked healthy.

Will: Didn't wake up one morning. She's not handling it well.

Tom: Well I'm sorry to hear that, we really liked them. And how are the grandkids?

Will: They have COVID. There's a new strain going around up north. Our daughter had to take the younger one to the E.R. and it's a good thing she did.

Tom: Why?

Will: They discovered he's anemic.

Tom: Waitress? Can we order? My friend here has to take off soon.

Waitress: Certainly. What can I get for you?

Tom: A vodka martini, two olives.

Will: I thought you were going to have the mahi-mahi?

Tom: I've lost my appetite.

Will: You might want to see a doctor. My cousin in Boca lost his about a month before he ... you know.

HAPPY BAY ISN'T

For two years I was a member of the board of directors of my community, Happy Bay (not its real name). I will explain how that came to pass a few paragraphs from now.

In the five years since my term ended, I have been plotting in my head a mystery novel tentatively titled *HOA*. Every Floridian who lives in a master planned community or condo — there are millions of us — knows HOA stands for Homeowners' Association.

> **HOA plot summary:** *HOA is set in Sunny Palms, a picturesque Florida community where the grass is always green (because if it isn't, you get fined). Most residents are retirees just looking to relax—except for the handful of people who treat litigation as a competitive sport.*
>
> *Trouble is brewing in paradise: A dissident group of residents is outraged when the community's billionaire developer announces plans to build a twenty thousand-square-foot McMansion on the HOA's private beach. The dissidents sue, the developer countersues, the HOA's board of directors gets dragged in, and soon, the only people making money are the lawyers. Residents take sides. Board meetings turn into scream fests. An anonymous email accuses the board president of taking bribes from the developer. The president denies it and sues the dissidents*

for defamation. The dissidents countersue because, well, why not? Eventually, the leader of the dissidents is found floating face-down in the golf course lake. Whodunnit? The board president? The developer? A resident tired of all the emails?

I had big plans for *HOA*. Hollywood would come knocking, aging stars would fight over roles, and I'd win an Oscar for the screenplay. But alas, I never wrote it.

I got the idea for HOA after running for my HOA's Board of Directors. I ran to put an end to a lawsuit that was dividing Happy Bay, costing a fortune, and making our community look like an episode of *Judge Judy*. That lawsuit was nothing like the one I envisioned for my book, but when my running mate and I won, it was settled.

And that was just beginning of my adventures as a board member. Here's a sampling of what I dealt with during my two-year term:

- **The Brawl**: An elderly owner claimed he was physically assaulted by the general manager. The GM claimed that he, not the owner, was the real victim. I was tasked with investigating. What the accuser didn't know was that a security camera had recorded the whole thing—showing him as the aggressor. When confronted with the footage, he declared it was *wrong* and demanded compensation. He got none.

- **The Great TV War**: Conservatives wanted CNN and MSNBC banned from the fitness center TVs. Liberals wanted to erase Fox News. After tense negotiations, we reached a compromise: HGTV, CNBC, and The Food Network.

- **Dementia Signs at the Gates**: As board liaison to the realtor community, I clashed with our publicity chair after she posted signs at all three entrances advertising a *Dementia Seminar for Residents*. My kids, who were visiting, thought it was hilarious. I did not. I asked her to put herself in the place of a realtor showing a home to potential buyers who might be a bit reluctant to buy in a community populated by demented zombies.

- **The Case of the Late Responder**: An owner threatened to sue the board president for not replying to his request within the exact timeframe specified in the bylaws. The president was halfway across the country tending to a dying family member at the time. After several one-on-one rants about how much he despised her (he even created a Facebook page demanding her removal), he graciously agreed to drop the matter *if* she issued a formal apology.

- **The Weeping Social Director**: A new social director, whose job was to plan events, turned out to be spectacularly unqualified. She failed to organize or promote any activities, and when questioned at a committee meeting, burst into tears, threw out her arms in crucifixion pose, and sobbed, *"This isn't a job—it's a crucifixion!"* She was fired.

- **Trivia Night Mutiny**: When our longtime Trivia Night host quit over a spat with the aforementioned social director, I begged him not to but he was adamant – he was done. I took over running it because I didn't want Happy Bay residents to lose one of their most popular activities. Immediately, rumors spread that I had *orchestrated his departure* because I wanted to run Trivia Night myself (as if I didn't have enough to do). Old people love conspiracy theories.

- **Grocery Store Grievances**: At Publix, I was often cornered by residents with urgent problems. One Ohio State alum insisted I force a Michigan fan to remove his Wolverines flag because HOA bylaws permitted only U.S. flags. (Technically, she was right.) I declined.
- **The Statue Scandal**: A homeowner was ordered to remove a lawn ornament (against the rules). She protested at an appeal hearing, only for me to later discover one of my fellow board members had the *exact same statue* on his porch. Awkward.
- **Pickleball Pandemonium**: Pickleball players demanded more courts. Zoning laws said no. The board proposed a new location; homeowners nearby objected to the noise. We hired a sound mitigation specialist; non-players objected to the cost. The result? Happy Bay still has the same six original courts, and they're more overcrowded than ever.

In total, I spent about five hours a week fulfilling my fiduciary duties. The other *thirty* hours? Dealing with absurd nonsensical crap that slowly wore me down.

Over my two-year term, I lost weight, lost sleep, and started dodging people in the supermarket. I was vilified in community-wide emails and became an expert at spotting residents who were about to ambush me with a complaint. I declined to run for a second term and have remained blissfully uninvolved in Happy Bay politics ever since.

The deadline to file for the next board election is three days away. Once again, Happy Bay is at war. A proposal to build a new recreation center was just defeated—not because it was a bad idea, but because an anonymous group (HOA's version of *QAnon*) spread emails claiming the board wasn't telling the truth about its true cost. Happy Bay remains frozen in time while neighboring communities modernize.

As I write this, none of the incumbent board members have filed for re-election.

Can't imagine why.

CUSTARD STORY

I dropped my daughter-in-law and grandkids off at the airport this morning. They have been visiting all week and were supposed to fly home yesterday but JetBlue canceled their flight, giving us an extra day to enjoy them.

We were out of food yesterday when we heard they would be staying longer than planned, so we took them to our local Culver's, the Wisconsin-based fast food chain known for hamburgers served on buttered buns, deep-fried cheese curds (one of my least favorite words), and frozen custard. As we were sitting in our booth, a message flashed on the closed-circuit TV screen Culver's uses to promote its menu: "Share your custard story."

This is my custard story but it's a story Culver's will never share on its social media pages or anywhere else. My mother, who heard this story from her mother, used to tell it, and it involves my great-grandparents, who were married in the eighteen-seventies. I'm not going to identify them by name. I don't want their fellow residents of Heaven to snicker behind their backs once they hear it, though I'm not above sharing this embarrassing tale if I omit their names.

Culver's patrons think of custard as a frozen dessert that comes out of a machine and is served in a cone or cup. My story is about an altogether different type of custard, a liquid concoction America's pioneers, including my great-grandparents' parents, made for special occasions like their daughter's wedding. It is made with heavy cream, egg yolks and sugar that is boiled together and served warm, in cups, on cold days. It is thick, meant to be sipped slowly, and tastes a bit like egg nog, but it's richer and creamier. Mom always made a pot or two every winter and buried the pressure cooker in which she made it in a snowbank, to keep it fresh so she could warm it up and enjoy it a few cups at a time. I didn't like mom's custard as a boy and, once I heard this story, never touched the stuff again. Here's the story:

At my great-grandparents' wedding reception in Mineola, Missouri, on a wintry night one hundred-fifty years ago, guests enjoyed fiddling, dancing, cake, and punchbowls filled with warm custard. The reception was, without doubt, the highlight of that year's social calendar in Mineola.

The groom, who was having a particularly good time, downed cup after cup of custard before he and his bride left for the new house he had built for them on his farm a few miles south of town.

In the middle of the night, the town's doctor was awakened by someone pounding on the door. It was the bride who had fled the farm on horseback. She was terribly upset. "Doctor, come quick. My husband is dying."

When the doctor arrived, he discovered the groom lying in bed. He had consumed so much custard that — there's no delicate way to say it — he had lost control of his bowels and squirted feces all over himself and the bed.

Whether the marriage had been consummated at this point I have no clue, but it's a safe bet to say that if it hadn't been, the groom couldn't have talked his new wife into it even if, after the doctor assured him he was going to live and he cleaned himself up, he wanted to get it on.

The best part of the story was the punchline my mother delivered which, no matter how many times we heard it, invariably sent our family into uncontrollable laughter. Mom delivered it in complete seriousness, intent on giving the impression she felt badly for the couple, but you just knew she was having trouble not bursting out into a raucous laugh herself: "Grandma suffered from depression her entire life."

If your spouse had done diarrhea all over the bed on your wedding night, you'd be depressed too.

Luckily for me and their other descendants, the bride wasn't so grossed out that she refused to allow her husband into their marriage bed ever again, because, over the next ten years, despite her melancholia, they had four children.

*

When we returned from Culver's, I called my sister and told her the restaurant chain was inviting customers to share their custard stories. "Do you think I should share our family's?"

"I don't think they'd publish it," she said.

"Mom always said … "I said slowly, the way mom used to draw it out for effect. She finished the sentence: "Grandma was depressed all her life!" We laughed until we couldn't laugh any more.

"What a shitty way to start your married life," my sister said. We laughed some more, and agreed that nobody — nobody — could tell a story better than our mother.

So that's my custard story.

As long as I've written it, I'm going to send it to Culver's, but I somehow doubt I'll be hearing from them.

HOLIDAY SONGS FOR TODAY

The second Trump administration promises that wokeness is dead. That remains to be seen. The following was written in 2021, when it was in full swing.

Have yourself a merry little Christmas

Have yourself a merry Festive Season,
Let your heart be light.
From now on
Our troubles will be out of sight
because CNN, *The New York Times*, WaPo, MSNBC and the
rest of the MSM refuse to report anything negative about
the inept Biden administration.

It's beginning to look a lot like Christmas

In the meadow we can build a snowman,
And pretend that he's that Fauci clown.
He'll ask, "Are you vaxxed?"
And we'll say "Sure Thing!
We got our jabs at CVS downtown."

Grandma got run over by a reindeer

Grandma got run over by a registered sex offender
who had just gotten out of jail on a thousand-dollar bond
for trying to
strangle his girlfriend
and now she's dead.

It's beginning to look a lot like Christmas

A pair of hopalong boots and a pistol that shoots
Is the wish of Janice and Jen.
Barbies that talk and will go for a walk
Is the hope of Barney and Ben.
And mom and dad can hardly wait
For school to start again
But it looks like there's a new COVID variant
So they'll probably resume remote learning.

The Christmas song

Chestnuts roasting on an open fire,
Jack Frost nipping at your bits.
Yuletide carols being sung by the fire,
And folks dressed up like Inuits.

Rudolph the red-nosed reindeer

Then one foggy Christmas Eve,
Santa came to say,
Rudolph with your nose so bright,
Won't you guide my sleigh tonight?
But Rudolph said no because Santa wouldn't provide him
with a helmet or allow him to work from home.

The first Noel

Noel, Noel, Noel, Noel,
Born is the king of racist, genocidal Israel.

You'd better watch out (for Alexa)

She hears you when you're sleeping
She knows when you go poo.
She knows if you've been bad or good
Tracking everything you do
which is why you're being bombarded with ads for Sleep
Number beds and ten-thousand-dollar Toto toilets.

Happy Festive Season (unless, of course, you don't celebrate in which case I hope you'll take no offense).

PERFECT EXECUTION

Florida is one of the few states that still carries out the death penalty on condemned criminals. Unfortunately, criminals who drive down I-75 for two-hundred miles with their blinkers on aren't among them.

I always read the news reports whenever an execution takes place at the state prison in Starke. I skip right over the inevitable aspects of every story — the condemned's last words, how he discovered God on death row, how many veins the doctor had to pierce to find one that could accommodate the IV drip, etc. — and go directly to what the guy ordered for his last meal.

I've thought a lot about what I would request for mine. Here's my list. I revise it regularly to keep it up-to-date in case I ever need it.

> **Kraft Dinner a la Stern:** Just so you're clear on this, I'm talking about the original blue vertical box with the skinny elbow macaroni, not the fancy stuff in the yellow box. I'd instruct the prison chef to prepare it using a trick from Jane and Michael Stern's *Square Meals*: Open two boxes, throw away the macaroni from one of them, prepare the noodles from the remaining box according to package directions, drain, then stir the foil packets containing the powdered "cheese" from *both* boxes into the noodles, along with twice

the butter and half the milk the recipe calls for. I would ask him to add two cans of Bumble Bee oil-packed tuna to the mixture. The ultimate comfort food for that long walk down the green mile.

Jet's Pizza: I always have to share with my wife so, for once, it would be nice to have my own entire pie from Jet's, a Detroit-based chain that has two storefronts near me. The crust is nothing special but the sauce, that incredible sauce, is beyond description. It's tomato-y and sweet, infused with herbs and spices that leave you drooling like a rabid raccoon. Realistically, I'd lick the sauce off, and leave the crust because I'd need room for …

Ravioli d'Oro: In Buenos Aires, my wife and I stumbled upon d'Oro, an Italian restaurant near the Casa Rosada. We walked out two hours later in a state of stupefaction, knowing we had just eaten the best meal of our lives. Specifically, handmade ravioli stuffed with Argentine grain-fed beef tenderloin, in a Malbec wine sauce. We discovered d'Oro on Friday and returned on Saturday. And Sunday. On Monday, our last night, it was closed. I wonder if the warden would fly the chef up? If the state refuses to pay his travel expenses, would my friends chip in? Hope so.

Pearl's peanut brittle: Pearl Houchins was an old lady and secretary of the Methodist Church in Auxvasse, Mo., where I grew up. Every Christmas, she made candy for the goodie bags that were passed out to the children of the church. She could have been a billionaire had she been willing to sell her recipes, which included an ethereally crispy, lighter-than-air peanut brittle, to Nestle, Mars or Hershey. But, to the eternal regret of those who knew only that she used hand-churned butter and fresh cream from local farmers, she took her recipes with her to heaven. No prison chef can possibly duplicate her version, so all I'll ask is that the warden have the head honcho from Mrs. See's Candies, which sells a decent peanut brittle, make mine using dairy products from zip code 65231.

Saganaki: As newlyweds we lived in Chicago where, every Saturday night, we ate in Greek Town, a two-block long row of restaurants west of the Loop. The best, hands-down, was (and still is) the Parthenon, where diners waited in line up to three hours. It was worth it for a single bite of the signature appetizer the Parthenon claims to have invented — saganaki, a slab of kasseri cheese, dredged in a secret coating and brought to the table in a cast iron skillet by a waiter who doused it with brandy, lit it with a lighter that caused the entire skillet to explode in flame, then extinguished the fire with the juice of a lemon as the crowd yelled, *"Oopa!"* I lie awake nights worrying about this particular request because I doubt the warden will allow the chef to light the dish in my presence lest I catch fire and deprive the state of the pleasure of frying my ass.

My wife's Chicken Parmigiana: OK, she uses Prego®, but who cares? Her version is tastier than anything any of those Italian TV chefs could conjure up. She might be sad as she prepares it but she'll take comfort knowing she'll soon be rich from the life insurance payout provided I'm executed no later than November 16, 2036, when the policy expires.

Stouffer's Chipped Beef: I'd instruct the chef to serve it over Pepperidge Farm Sourdough toast, topped by two slices of Velveeta that melt when they come in contact with the bubbling cream sauce. I'd also request a mill of fresh pepper to grind liberally over the entire plate.

Blondies from the corner deli: When we lived in Manhattan B.C. — Before Children — a deli on the corner of 49th and Second sold blondies so rich it took an hour to consume one 3-in. x 3-in. x 1-in. square. Imagine a slice of gooey butter cake studded with semi-sweet chocolate morsels and you'll have a rough idea of what I'm talking about here. A full bite would have sent anyone into a sugar- and butter-induced nirvana from which there could be no return. The only possible way to eat one was to break off a fingernail-sized piece, suck out the butter, then let the rest melt in your mouth. The blondies were made by the deli owner's wife in an apartment kitchen in Queens, and delivered every evening around 8 p.m. Sometimes they were still warm. Next to the twin towers, those blondies are what I miss most about New York.

Lottie Gasper's Fried Chicken: During my college summers, I worked the night shift at Gasper's Truck Plaza in Kingdom City, Mo., where, for two-dollars forty-nine cents, truckers could get a breast, drumstick and wing of the world's crispiest fried chicken, accompanied by mashed potatoes, white cream gravy with flecks of crust from the skillet in which the chicken was fried, and canned green beans, served up on a plate festooned with a ring of candied crabapple and a piece of lettuce. I ate it at 4:30 every morning for four straight summers and it's probably the reason I have to take statins to control my cholesterol today Gasper's, alas is long gone but surely someone who worked in the kitchen remembers Miss Lottie's recipe. Anyone? I'll let you know the address of the prison warden to send it to.

I wonder if he'll let me have seconds if I ask nicely?

GUNNAR AND GERDA
MOVE TO FLORIDA

I love those HGTV reality shows that feature couples shopping for homes. There are a number of variations, but all follow the same formula. A couple with polar-opposite ideas about what they want visits three homes with a real estate agent. The agent, as they bicker — these couples argue so much they shouldn't live on the same continent much less under the same roof — keeps reminding them they are making her job damn near impossible. At the end of each episode, the couple chooses one of the homes, which never meets the criteria they told the agent they wanted at the beginning. Some episodes feature newlyweds looking for condos in big cities like Philadelphia or Chicago. Others follow couples with kids shopping for suburban homes with plenty of space for their growing families.

My favorite house hunters are couples nearing retirement age looking for homes in Florida where they can live out their golden years. The wife, inevitably, wants a home that's up-to-date or brand new, so she won't have to worry about choosing paint colors or tiles and can jump right into learning mahjong. The husband wants a fixer-upper. He is convinced a home that needs renovation will not only save money, it will give him something to do in retirement. He tells the agent how much they are willing to spend and warns her not to show homes that exceed his budget. The wife tells the agent to feel free to show them more expensive properties because, after all these years, she knows she married a cheapskate.

Nobody talks like the house hunters on these shows. The couples and their agents are, clearly, reading from scripts. I read somewhere that in many cases the couples have already decided on a home before taping begins, so the show is bogus from the get-go.

Here's a script for a Florida retirement house-hunting show I'd like to see.

Gunnar and Gerda Move to Florida

Voiceover (*as a map appears with a line being drawn from Fargo, North Dakota, to Florida*): After four decades running their dry-cleaning business in frigid Fargo, North Dakota, Gunnar and Gerda Svensen are seeking a home in sunny Naples, Florida, where they can enjoy their well-earned retirement.

(*Cut to quick shots of Gunnar and Gerda as they stroll hand-in-hand down Fifth Avenue in Naples. They walk into a real estate office, and sit with an agent. The three chat animatedly as the voiceover continues.*)

They have enlisted real estate agent Susie Green to find them a home within their budget of two hundred fifty-thousand dollars. Susie has her work cut out for her because Gunnar and Gerda have vastly different concepts of what their new home should be. Gunnar is dreaming of a condo in a golf-course community that needs renovations he can do himself. He is willing to put in sweat equity, knowing it will make their budget go further and give him something to do when he isn't sitting at the Nineteenth Hole. Gerda has her heart set on a spacious high-rise penthouse overlooking one of Naples' beautiful beaches...with an open-concept living/dining/family room...an up-to-date kitchen with industrial-grade appliances...and a terrace featuring a skating rink their hockey-loving twin grandsons, Leo and Lars, can use when they visit.

(*Cut to Susie, Gunnar, and Gerda standing in front of the door of a home they are about to enter.*)

Susie (*opening door, gesturing for her clients to enter and look around*): Well, what do you think?

Gerda: This isn't a house, it's a trailer.

Susie: It's a mobile home.

Gerda: I don't want a house on wheels.

Susie: You'll be glad for those wheels when a hurricane is headed this way. Just hook it up to the back of your truck and pull it across Alligator Alley to the other coast, where it will be out of harm's way.

Gerda (*looking down in horror*): That turquoise carpet is gross! I hate carpet.

Susie: I'm told there is linoleum underneath but I'm not sure what shape it's in. I'm guessing it's the original floor from the fifties when this home came off the assembly line.

Gunnar: I like the orange walls with the palm tree decals. Very tropical! How many bedrooms does this place have?

Susie: One.

Gerda: Where will the twins sleep when they come to visit?

Susie: There's a pull-out couch in the living room. Or you could buy one of those inflatable mattresses, it's up to you.

Gerda: How many bathrooms?

Susie: None, but you'll have access to toilets and showers in the community center whenever you need them.

Gunnar: How much is this?

Susie: The mobile home is seventy-nine thousand dollars.

Gunnar: Yah, I like that!

Susie: I'm not finished. The pad it's parked on is three hundred fifty-nine thousand.

Gunnar: Gosh darn it! This whole place — the trailer and the lot — would sell for three grand in Fargo.

Susie: Well, that's the price you pay for a Naples address.

Gerda: We're not in Naples. This dump is in the middle of the Everglades.

Susie: This mobile home park has a Naples address, and that alone is worth a quarter of a million.

Gunnar: Well, you have certainly given us something to think about. What else do you have to show us?

Susie: You're really going to fall in love with the next place.

(COMMERCIAL BREAK)

(Quick cuts of footage from the previous segment, showing the trio visiting home number one.)

Voiceover: Gunnar and Gerda just looked at a home in a historic neighborhood in prestigious Naples, Florida. While it does have a roof, it doesn't have everything else they are looking for in their Florida forever home. Today, Susie is taking them to see another home.

Susie: You're really going to fall in love with the next place.

(Cut to Susie, Gunnar, and Gerda walking on a dock at Naples' Tin City marina. They stop in front of a boat. Seagulls

are circling overhead. One drops guano on the front of Gunnar's aloha shirt.)

Gunnar: I'm gonna have to dry clean this when we go back north to pack.

Susie: You're really going to fall in love with the next place.

Gerda: I don't mean to be rude, but that's the third time you've said that.

Susie: I know. The directors never have enough footage for a twenty-one-minute show, so they splice shots of agents repeating ourselves again and again. They assume people who binge-watch these shows won't remember what they just saw because they all run together after a while.

Gunnar: What the heck is this?

Susie: A seventy-eight-foot houseboat. I know Gerda wants to be on the water.

Gunnar: It doesn't look like a houseboat.

Susie: Well, for twenty years it was used as a shrimp boat...

Gerda: Like the one in *Forrest Gump*?

Susie: ...but the seller converted it into a houseboat last year. It has four berths...

Gerda: That's wonderful for when the boys visit.

Susie: ... a dinette, head, sink, shower, microwave, and a freezer that can flash-freeze up to four tons of fresh shrimp.

Gerda: I don't want to live on a boat. I'd get seasick. And that smell. *(She holds her nose.)* It's nauseating.

Gunnar: How much?

Susie: It comes in right under your budget at two hundred forty-nine thousand dollars.

Gunnar: There's definite potential here. But we don't want to commit until we see one more place.

(COMMERCIAL BREAK)

Voiceover *(as Susie, Gunnar, and Gerda exit an SUV parked in the circular driveway of a two-story mansion)*: Today, Susie is taking Gunnar and Gerda to a home in Naples' tony Port Royal neighborhood.

Gerda: Now this is more like it!

(Susie opens the front door and, sweeping her arm, gestures for them to go inside. They walk into an enormous foyer with double curved staircases leading to the second floor.)

Susie: I saved the best for last. This place is brand new with twenty-thousand square feet and two hundred-fifty feet of bay-front footage. There are three air-conditioned garages to accommodate up to twelve cars and the dock has a guest house, fire pit and party bar.

Gerda: I love it! *(The trio walks through an empty ballroom-size space.)*

Susie: The couple who had it built spared no expense. They wanted a house large enough for their adult children and grandkids when they came to visit and for their live-in staff. Unfortunately, they passed away before it was complete. *(They enter the kitchen area and pause at one of the two islands. Gerda runs her hand approvingly over the countertop.)*

Gerda: I absolutely love this spacious open-concept living/dining/family room and this beautiful kitchen with its quartz countertops, Italian cabinetry and industrial-grade professional appliances.

Gunnar: How many bedrooms?

Susie: Eighteen, all of them *en-suite*.

Gerda: We only need four — one for us, one for our daughter and her husband, and one each for the twins.

Susie: All those extra bedrooms will come in handy when your Fargo friends come to visit in the winter months. Here's the first guest bedroom. *(Susie opens a door, and Gerda peers into the room and looks down.)*

Gerda: Ugh, carpet again. I told you I don't like carpet.

Susie: Handwoven in Persia just for this room, and it's the only carpet in the house. If you don't like it, no problem, you can remove it — there's hardwood underneath, a rare mahogany from Mozambique in a lovely herringbone pattern.

Gerda: How far are we from shopping and restaurants?

Susie: Less than two miles to Fifth Avenue with its plethora of fine dining, boutiques, wealth advisers, and two hundred-plus real estate offices.

(Gunnar peers out the window. Cut to a lavish pool with multiple water features and a bikini-clad blonde on a chaise lounge, sipping a cocktail.)

Gunnar: Does she come with the house?

Susie *(chuckling)*: That's the head housekeeper. And yes, she comes with the house.

Gerda: Where's the ice-skating rink for the twins?

Susie: You can always have one built.

Gunnar: What's the asking price?

Susie: Thirty-four million.

Gunnar: Who can afford that?

Susie: Everyone in Naples but you.

Gunnar: Is the price negotiable?

Susie *(laughing)*: You'll never know until you ask!

Gerda: Looks like we have a decision to make.

(COMMERCIAL BREAK)

(Gunnar and Gerda at a wine bar, deep in conversation.)

Gunnar: I really liked the orange walls in house number one. House two — the boat? It came in on budget, but I'm not so sure about that one.

Gerda: The fish smell was awful. We'd never get rid of it. Since the director said we have to eliminate one and act like it was an excruciating decision, let's cross that off.

Gunnar: Agreed.

(They clink wine glasses.)

Gerda: That leaves two. I know what we should do.

Gunnar: Yeah, me too. What shall we tell Susie?

(COMMERCIAL BREAK)

(Quick cuts of Gunnar and Gerda from previous segments, exploring the three homes.)

Voiceover: Gunnar and Gerda want to spend their golden years in beautiful Naples, Florida. Their realtor, Susie, has shown them three homes. House number one is priced over their two hundred fifty-thousand-dollar budget, and both agree it has issues. Home number two is a houseboat with the basics they need and a freezer for up to four tons of shrimp, but it, too, has issues. They eliminated it from consideration before the commercial break, but the director tells me I need to fill fifteen seconds, so I'm repeating it again. The third home has almost everything they want except an ice-skating rink. Gerda loves it, but Gunnar isn't so sure — it is more than thirty-three million over budget. *(Cut to Gunnar and Gerda in wine bar.)*

Gunnar: What shall we tell Susie?

Gerda: We should tell her we have a perfectly lovely house on two acres in Fargo that's paid for and just appraised for two hundred fifty-thousand. It has five bedrooms and baths, a sauna, gym, and a pond that's frozen solid nine months of the year for the twins. After seeing what we'd get for our money in Naples, I plan to stay in it until they come carry my dead body away.

Gunnar: I couldn't agree more. Let's call Susie and tell her. *(They stand up and walk away from the table.)* *(Cut to Susie at her desk.)*

Susie: I have to admit I was disappointed. But I'm confident that if Gunnar and Gerda decide to resume their search, I can find them something they'll love.

(Credits roll.)

ARE YOU OFFICIALLY ELDERLY?

Today's news reports that an elderly man, 61, was struck and killed while crossing U.S. 41 in Ft. Myers. Unfortunate? Absolutely. But *elderly*? Not in my book. At seventy-three, I consider a guy his age to be a man-child — old enough to ~~cross the street on his own~~ remember the days when there were only two sexes, but so young he wasn't eligible for Medicare.

You may delude yourself into thinking you're not elderly, but at some point, between the time you actually do get that coveted Medicare card and the time your corpse is loaded in the cargo hold of a plane to take your remains up north, you slowly but surely will attain that status. Here are twenty-five sure signs you've officially qualified as elderly.

- Thumbing through *People* in the supermarket checkout line, the only celebrities you recognize are listed on the "In Memoriam" page.
- People who look much older than you say, "Thank you sir" when you hold the door open for them.
- All your shoes are Skechers.
- The happy couples in the erectile dysfunction commercials look thirty years younger than you.

- You go to Dunkin' — you still call it Dunkin' Donuts even though the name changed in 2019 — and order a large coffee. The counterperson asks what kind of donut you want. You say you don't want a donut. He informs you seniors are entitled to a free donut with a large coffee.
- You haven't bought a new suit in ten years.
- A TV show stars an actor you haven't seen recently. You can't believe how old and decrepit he looks. He's about your age, he should look better than that. You look him up on Wikipedia and learn he is fourteen years younger than you.
- You're the only person you know who still has a landline. Only your kids and robo-callers call on it. You've been meaning to have it disconnected but haven't because you have to provide your phone number every time you go to a supermarket, drugstore, convenience store or gas station to earn loyalty points (even though you're not sure what, if anything, you are getting for those points) and it would be too much hassle to have to explain to clerks that you need to change it to your cell phone number.
- You tear up when "Cat's in the Cradle" comes on the radio because you identify with the guy singing it.
- Your niece just retired.
- Your other niece is having cataract surgery.
- You tell Alexa "thank you" every time she answers a question. You feel stupid for doing it — she's a robot for Chrissakes — but can't help yourself: Your parents taught you to thank people who do something nice for you.
- You refuse to pay a dollar for a single potato because you remember when a five-pound bag cost forty-nine cents.

- You are seeing ads from the Cremation Society on the internet.
- You go to a Kenny Loggins concert and half the audience is wearing oxygen tanks.
- As Kenny is singing *The House at Pooh Corner* you realize you forgot to drink your Metamucil.
- You were always amused by friends who took sweaters to restaurants complaining the A/C was too cold but now you do, too.
- You refuse to go to any venue that features live music because it makes your hearing aids screech.
- When your new personal trainer asks your fitness goal, you tell him, if you are a man, that you want to get your butt back because it has mysteriously disappeared. If you are a woman, you tell him you want to shrink your butt.
- You're one hundred-fifty pages into a book before you realize you've already read it.
- Friends your age are constantly forwarding emails about how swell things were back in the good old days when kids could drink from garden hoses without getting sick and didn't have to wear bike helmets or seat belts. They think you remember those days. You do.
- Hotel clerks ask if you need a room near the elevator so you won't have to walk so far.
- As you are following a Buick down the highway, the jukebox in your head suddenly goes off, playing an advertising jingle from your youth: *Wouldn't you really rather have a Buick? A Buick, sixty-five Buick. Wouldn't you really rather have a Buick … than any other car this year?*

- The day before a hurricane is forecast to arrive, you decide to use your chainsaw to remove the palm fronds brushing against your pool cage that damaged the screens during the last hurricane. You tell your wife you need her to hold the ladder for you. She refuses, saying someone your age has no business being up on a ladder because you're going to fall and break your hip or decapitate yourself or her. When she leaves, you do it anyway and sawdust gets in your eyes because you didn't wear protective goggles. The pain is excruciating and when she gets home she has to drive you to the emergency eye clinic. Not that I know anyone this has happened to.

- Because you have nothing better to do, you decide to count the number of bullet points in this chapter to see if Dryden really listed 25 reasons or if he's cheating you.

ARE YOUR GENITALS
THE ONES
YOU WERE BORN WITH?

Saturday night, my wife and I were watching TV. Suddenly I felt a throbbing pain in my left shoulder. It felt like I was being stabbed with an ice pick.

As everyone — especially folks my age — should, I've committed to memory the symptoms of a heart attack. A sudden pain in the chest and/or arms and/or shoulder is one of the biggies. There were no other symptoms — no sweating, nausea or shortness of breath — but the pain was God-awful. One minute I was fine. The next I was doubled over. A half-hour later, after Tylenol failed to relieve even an iota of the pain, I went to the E.R.

A few years ago, following a colonoscopy, I wrote a blog post pointing out how ridiculous it is that medical workers are now required to ask every patient the same two questions. Every person I encountered that day, from the receptionist to the doctor, asked me 1) my name and 2) birthdate. Apparently, they suspected I might be one of those whack jobs with Munchausen syndrome, posing as a patient I knew was scheduled to undergo the procedure that day. Judging from the way I was repeatedly interrogated, they must have suspected I had drugged him, left him tied up in a closet, and showed up to the hospital in his place because I adore having colonoscopies and all the attention I knew he would get.

I was informed it was a rule. They had to ask those questions of every patient.

Saturday night, everyone at the E.R. — the attendant who put me in a wheel chair and rushed me to the exam room, the clerk who asked for my insurance cards, the attending physician, the radiology technician — asked those same stupid questions. And as I was lying on a gurney with my shirt off, waiting for an EKG, a nurse asked another question. "Are your genitals the ones you were born with?"

I was gobsmacked. For starters, the question ended with a preposition. She should have known better. Secondly, my genitals were covered by my shorts and I can't imagine I was giving off vibes that would have given her any reason to doubt I was an ordinary seventy-something male with his original genitals; I had washed off my mascara and removed my favorite leopard-print bra before I left for the E.R. Last but not least, I hadn't come to the E.R. because I was having a problem with that part of my anatomy so what difference did it make if, in fact, mine weren't original? Asking a heart attack patient about his genitals is as ridiculous as asking someone with a broken leg about his tonsils.

"Why are you asking me this?"

She replied it's a new rule, a question the hospital requires workers to ask every patient exhibiting systems of a coronary event. She said the protocol for treating male heart attack victims is different from the procedure the hospital is supposed to follow for women. Not wanting to delay the treatment I was sure I needed to survive, I said, "Yes, I'm almost sure they are." But maybe I was wrong. To be honest, I don't remember anything from the day I was born. A nurse at the hospital could have pulled a fast one and switched mine with some other newborn's.

I have since thought of smart-ass answers I could have provided.

"No, the ones I was born with were much smaller."

"Last time I looked they were."

"No, I cut my original genitals off with a chainsaw while I was tripping on acid and the ones I have now are plastic."

"I'm not sure. You're the medical professional. Why don't you take a look and you tell me?"

After a thorough examination which, I couldn't help but note, excluded my genitals which may or may not be original, the doctor gave me a muscle relaxer and pain pill and ordered blood tests, X-rays and a CAT scan.

When the results came back, I was relieved to learn I wasn't experiencing a heart attack. It was a shoulder spasm. The doc said ligaments had suddenly seized up and tightened around the muscles in my shoulder, like a noose around the neck of a condemned man being hanged. (Or should I say hung?) The likely cause was arthritis, a condition I didn't know I had. He asked if I had ever injured my shoulder or collarbone and said that, if so, that might be the cause of the arthritis. While I don't remember the incident, my mother always told me that, when my genitals were covered by a diaper, I broke my collarbone falling out of my high chair. Mystery solved.

The doctor prescribed a week of steroids and stretching exercises. Three hours after I walked in sure I was about to die, I went home.

Although the shoulder still hurts, I am feeling much better, but now I am worried. I wish my mother or the doctor who delivered me were alive. If so, either would be able to provide a definitive answer to the question the nurse asked but both are gone, so I guess I'll never know for sure.

OBITUARY:
BILLY RAY DRYDEN

Billy Ray Dryden went to be with Jesus on July 20, 2018. Moments after greeting him at the pearly gates Jesus is reported to have announced, "I can't deal with this nonstop barking," and took off for parts unknown.

Billy was born August 22, 2003, in Pomfret Center, Conn. On November 22 of that year, he was adopted by Judith and Thomas Dryden. He rarely acknowledged his father; Billy was, heart and soul, from the moment he was placed in her arms as a two-pound puppy, his mama's boy. Their love for one another was pure and unconditional. Billy could do no wrong in his mother's eyes, even when he hiked his leg on her baby grand. For nearly fifteen years he was tucked under her arm twenty-four hours a day.

As those who knew him will attest, Billy was vocal. He barked at thunder. He barked at lightning. He barked at fireworks. He barked when the phone or doorbell rang. He barked when a phone or doorbell on TV rang. He barked at the pool man, the yard men, at postal workers and at delivery people. He barked at his neighbors George and Mary. He barked at children. He barked at adults. He barked at other dogs, at lizards on the lanai, and at birds and planes. He barked especially loud whenever his father attempted to hold a conversation with his mother.

He loved Costco rotisserie chicken, frolicking through the snow of his native Connecticut, and riding in the car where he always slept on his mother's lap, the one time his parents could talk to each other without having to scream.

Billy was a hero. One day he discovered that a miniature shark his human brother Stuart had adopted years before — a fish that was supposed to live for a year or two but was six years old at that point — had somehow leapt out of the aquarium and landed behind a chair. Billy began barking. His mother paid no notice since Billy barked constantly, but his barking became increasingly agitated, and she saw he was trying to paw his way under the chair. She realized he was telling her something. His mother was able to pick up the shark with a spatula and slip it back into the fish tank. The shark, alas, suffered brain damage because, from that day until his death several years later, he could only swim counter-clockwise, but his life was saved thanks to the bravery and persistence of a nine-pound long-haired black-and-English cream dachshund.

Billy was predeceased by his dachshund sister, Bonnie, who tricked him out of his breakfast every day for years by standing at the door barking, pretending to see something in the yard, which always made him run to the door where he would bark at nothing for ten minutes as she doubled back and inhaled his food. Not surprisingly, Bonnie was overweight whereas Billy remained rail-thin. Other survivors include his dachshund brother, Rupert, whom he welcomed into the family after Bonnie's death and loved dearly; his mongrel Great Pyrenees/Greyhound bitch of a niece Topanga, whom he despised, especially after she tried to swallow him whole under the Christmas tree when he stole the toy Santa had brought her; his father; and the love of his life and reason for being, his mother.

Billy was cremated and, at his mother's request, the red lacquer box in which his ashes were returned will someday be placed alongside her body in her coffin, so they can spend eternity the same way they spent their life on earth together — with him tucked safely under her arm.

A TEXT FROM MEGAN

+1 971 555 4824   Thurs, Apr. 5 at 9:37 PM

Why can't I reach u on yr phone? Did u block me?

Who is this?

This is Megan

The only Megan I know is 4. She doesn't have a phone

LOL! Of course you know me. We met at Jessie's party.

I don't know any Jessie

We talked for hours then u came back to my place

I did?

U R bad! Love yr sense of humor.
Before u left u gave me your number

Where are you?

At work but I'm thinking about
stopping on my way home for a glass
of wine. Wanna meet up?

I can't

I keep thinking about u. I felt a real
connection.

OK

I've left messages but u never call
back

You're texting from area code
971. Where is that?

Portland

Oregon or Maine?

LOL. Oregon silly!

Never been there

Hahaha. Where r u?

Florida

I remember u said u travel a lot for work. What are u doing down there?

Watching TV

What are u watching?

The Bear on Hulu. My wife wanted to watch it

WTF!!!! U r married??? How long?

49 years

OMG! Who am I talking to?

Tom

You're not Justin! Why didn't u say something???

I tried

How old are u?

73

I'm sooo embarrassed. Sorry to bother u. I'll double check the number next time

No problem

Enjoy The Bear. I loved it.

Mind if I ask you a question?

Sure, go ahead

Can I take a raincheck in case I ever get to Portland?

F U!!!!!!!!

BECOMING UNGLUED

I have done many things I'm ashamed of.

I tipped the valet at a fancy restaurant one dollar when I meant to give him five.

I brought brownies frosted with ExLax to a goodbye party for someone I was glad to see go.

During the first month of the COVID lockdown, I watched three seasons — thirty-nine back-to-back episodes — of *90-Day Fiancé* on TLC. Each episode was ninety minutes long. That's two days and ten hours of my life I'll never get back.

All these questionable deeds reflected poor judgment on my part but none were crimes *per se*. You are about to read the story of something I did that definitely was a crime. Now that the statute of limitations has expired and I can't be charged for committing it, I am confessing my crime to the readers of this book.

In April, 1983, our first son was two months old. I was a copywriter for an ad agency in Manhattan, where we lived in a tiny one-bedroom co-op with the baby and our two neurotic dachshunds, Sybil and Quincy. S & Q barked LOUD ENOUGH TO WAKE THE DEAD whenever the doorbell rang, causing the foul-tempered British couple in the apartment below to pound the ceiling with a broomstick and shout epithets signaling their displeasure.

Throughout the pregnancy, we were planning to raise the baby in our shoebox-in-the-sky. We loved living in New York, but couldn't afford a two-bedroom apartment. A few weeks after bringing him home, we were ready to move — there simply wasn't enough room for the three of us, all that baby paraphernalia, and the dogs.

One morning I called a friend in Connecticut and asked him to hook us up with his realtor. That afternoon we signed an offer to buy a Norwalk condo containing not just two but three bedrooms, two full baths, an honest-to-God dining room and a kitchen with drawers and a four-burner stove.

Two weeks before we were to close on the new place, my wife arranged for movers to visit our apartment and give us a quote. When I left for work that morning, she reminded me they were coming at 7 p.m. I promised I would be home to meet with them.

Uh-oh. I had to work late on a last-minute project for an industrial adhesive company called Loctite that was due to the client first thing the next day. Loctite had developed the super-strength adhesive I was writing about for Boeing to use in place of rivets on its planes. The adhesive was applied with a device that looked like a hypodermic needle. I was on my second Tanqueray and tonic — Tanqueray was another client and everyone in the agency was free to drink it after hours. I had a nice buzz going, and was almost finished writing, when the phone rang.

It was my wife. She was upset. "The movers rang the doorbell and, as usual, the dogs started barking. A minute later, as the moving men were looking around the apartment, there was a knock on the door. The dogs started up again. It was that awful English woman downstairs. She started screaming about your 'fucking dogs' and how 'sick of the goddam noise' she was. She's going to go to the co-op board and demand we get rid of them."

"You go downstairs and tell her she won't have to hear them much longer because we're moving," I told her.

A few minutes later she called back, sobbing. "I took the baby, went downstairs, knocked on the door, and the husband answered. Before I could say anything, he pointed at the baby … sneered, 'I feel sorry for him with you as his mother' … and slammed the door. I had to jump back so it wouldn't hit the baby."

"I'll be right home," I said, throwing on my overcoat. I slipped a Loctite hypodermic needle into my pocket and ran the ten blocks to our building.

I got off the elevator on the floor below ours, injected the Loctite adhesive into the locks and between the metal door and door frame of the British couple's apartment, and tossed the hypodermic needle down the trash chute.

My wife had calmed down when I got home. "I feel better. I over-reacted. My hormones are still out of whack."

I told her what I had done. She was horrified.

The next morning we heard a commotion from the apartment below. The couple was pounding on their door, yelling, "Help, we're trapped! Get us out!"

I rode the elevator down one flight. When its door opened and I looked down the hall, the building superintendent was outside the couple's door, assuring them help was on the way. I hightailed it back upstairs and told my wife, "Let's get out of here." We put the baby in his carriage, leashed the dogs, and fled.

Neighbors later told us the NYFD had to blowtorch a hole through the door to free the couple.

That night as we were returning, we ran into the Brits in the building's lobby. "We're going to sue your ass," the man told us. "What are you talking about?" I replied. "The cement in our locks!" the woman snarled. At that moment I remembered: They were both lawyers. *Shit.*

The next morning I paid a visit to my attorney, a friend who practiced with his father. I told him what I had done. He insisted I repeat the story for his dad, who, when he heard it, roared with laughter. "If you get sued and we represent you, I want you to pay us with that Loctite stuff. There are lot of people I'd like to do that to."

Turning serious, the elder attorney said that, if the couple could prove I had done it — and because I had left no fingerprints on the door and thrown the needle down the trash chute into the incinerator, it would be difficult — I could be charged with false imprisonment, vandalism and a couple of other crimes I've tried to forget. He said my wife and I should stay away from shabbily-dressed men who came up to us on the street because one could be a process server.

Happily, we didn't run into the Brits or any process servers, shabbily-dressed or otherwise, before the movers came and took us away to our new suburban home.

After all these years, I feel better for finally getting this off my chest. Glad you were here for me.

CHICKEN NOODLE SOUP

Time: 6:30 pm Sunday.

Place: The booth opposite ours in a fifties-themed diner.

Cast of characters: A forty-something waitress, a sixty-ish woman, and a man in his late eighties or early nineties whose walker is parked next to the booth.

Waitress: Are you ready to order?

Woman: I am but my father here needs a little more time.

Waitress: No rush, I'll be back in a minute. *(She leaves.)*

Woman *(to father, who is thumbing through a multi-page menu)*: Dad, it's a diner, you can get anything you want. Meat loaf, chicken, fish, a nice steak, a burger, you can even have breakfast. Would you like some scrambled eggs and bacon? Or some pancakes?

Old man *(flipping through the menu)*: Why's this menu's so damn big?

Woman: They even have liver and onions, your favorite.

Old man: I don't want it.

Woman: Well, what sounds good?

Old man: Nothing. I'm not hungry. Why did you bring me here when I'm not hungry? I get all the food I want at (a nearby retirement home).

Woman: I thought you might enjoy getting out, eating something different, spending some time together.

Old man: Well I'm not enjoying myself. You order for me.

Waitress *(returning with pad in hand)*: Have you decided?

Woman: I'll have the grilled grouper.

Waitress: What kind of dressing on your salad?

Woman: Balsamic.

Waitress *(to man)*: And you, sir?

Old man *(indicating his daughter)*: Ask her.

Woman *(to her father)*: Well, dad, if you aren't hungry, how about a bowl of soup?

Old man: If you say so.

Woman *(to waitress)*: What's your soup of the day?

Waitress: Tonight's special is tomato rice. We also have our famous chili, beef and barley, vegetable, minestrone, lemon orzo and chicken noodle.

Old man: Bring me the chicken noodle but I don't want any noodles in it.

Waitress: No problem at all. I'll ladle it up myself then go through it and remove the noodles.

(Twenty minutes later, as woman and man are eating.)

Waitress: Are we good here?

Woman: Yes, thank you.

Old man: Why in the hell did you say "we?" You're not eating with us.

Waitress *(ignoring the insult, sweetly addressing man)*: And how's your chicken noodle soup?

Old man: There aren't any noodles in it!

Woman *(to man, gently)*: Dad, you told her you didn't want noodles. This nice lady went through your soup and took them all out.

Old man: Why would I say that?

Woman: I don't know.

Old man: You heard me wrong. What kind of restaurant serves chicken noodle soup and leaves out the noodles?

Woman: I'm sorry, he's not usually like this.

Old Man *(accusingly to waitress)*: I don't get it. You're selling chicken noodle soup with no noodles!

Woman *(to waitress, sounding exhausted)*: Actually, yes, he is like this all the time.

Waitress *(sympathetically)*: That's okay, I understand.

Old man: I've had chicken noodle soup on every goddamn continent and I've never once been served chicken noodle soup without noodles.

Woman *(to waitress)*: I'm so sorry.

Waitress: I'll be back with your check in a minute.

Old man *(to waitress)*: You don't expect me to pay for this soup, do you?

Waitress: No sir, I'll take it off the bill. I'm sorry you didn't like it.

Old man: Well, it wasn't half bad. Except there weren't any noodles in it.

BANK FRAUD HOTLINE

Bank Call Center Rep: (BCCR): Thank you for calling (Bank Name) Fraud Department. To whom do I have the pleasure of speaking today?

TD: Thomas Dryden. I just got a text that someone tried to use my Visa card in Europe.

BCCR: Alright Mr. Thomas, I see you are calling from the phone number we have on record for you. Can you tell me your password?

TD: Dachshund. That's d-a-c-h-s-h-u-n-d.

BCCR: So, you are saying you didn't attempt to charge twenty-three thousand five-hundred euros at the Casino de Monte-Carlo in Monaco twelve minutes ago?

TD: I'm at home. And I'm holding my card. It hasn't been out of my possession.

BCCR: Well, Mr. Thomas, here is what we will do. We'll open an investigation, cancel your current card, and issue a new card with a different number. It will arrive in eight to ten days.

TD: This is the fourth time this year this has happened. I must have at least a dozen accounts on auto-pay — my cable, gym, cell phone, Netflix, and others. Am I going to have to contact them and give them the new number?

BCCR: Unfortunately yes, Mr. Thomas.

TD: Is there any way you can get the new card to me faster?

BCCR: We can send it express mail. You'll have it by Tuesday, Wednesday at the latest.

TD: Thanks, that's doable. And thanks for notifying me about the fraud. Good catch.

BCCR: As long as I have you on the phone, Mr. Thomas, can we review some more pending charges to your card?

TD: Sure.

BCCR: Yesterday at 7:37 p.m., fifty dollars ninety-eight cents at CVS, Naples, Florida.

TD: That's legit. Allergy meds.

BCCR: Saturday at 7:24 p.m., seven hundred forty-two euros to Madame XXX and her Nubile Nymphets, Amsterdam.

TD: How could I have been in Amsterdam at the same time I was in Florida? That's not mine.

BCCR: Alright Mr. Thomas, we will mark that as suspicious. How about Saturday at 5.02 p.m., thirty-nine dollars and one cent at Exxon Mobil in Estero, Florida?

TD: Legit.

BCCR: Saturday at 2:25 p.m., one hundred ninety-two dollars and seventy-six cents at Rocky Mountain High Cannabis Dispensary, Boulder, Colorado.

TD: That's not mine, either.

BCCR: Alright Mr. Thomas, we will investigate that charge.

TD: I haven't been to Colorado this decade.

BCCR: Friday at 10:11 a.m., thirty-nine dollars and twelve cents at Ace Hardware, Bonita Springs, Florida.

TD: That's legit.

BCCR: Thursday at 6:19 p.m., twenty-seven dollars and seventeen cents at Publix Supermarket, Bonita Springs, Florida.

TD: That's legit, too.

BCCR: Thursday at 4:42 p.m., four hundred-sixty Singaporean dollars at Raffles Bar, Singapore.

TD: No. Unfortunately.

BCCR: I beg your pardon?

TD: It's not legit.

BCCR: Thursday at 3:54 p.m., forty-four dollars at Pet Smart, Estero, Florida.

TD: That's a real one.

BCCR: Okay Mr. Thomas, I see that all other charges took place in Florida and have already been posted to your account, so they are legitimate. Allow up to forty-eight hours for delivery of your new card.

TD: I'll be looking for it.

BCCR: Thank you for calling (Bank Name). Is there anything else I can do for you?

TD: Yes.

BCCR: What is that, Mr. Thomas?

TD: If you ever find him, introduce me to the guy who made those charges. He's having more fun than I am.

DRIVING IN FLORIDA

Comedians love joking about geriatric Florida drivers. Their refusal to use turn signals. Their insistence, when driving on freeways, on occupying the far-left lane with their car's cruise control set to fifty miles-per-hour, parallel to another driver in the center lane whose vehicle is also traveling fifty miles-per-hour, making it impossible for anyone to pass, a situation which, on January 13, 2024, caused a five-hundred seventy-nine-mile back-up on I-95 from Jupiter to Florence, South Carolina.

You, of course, will not be one of those dangerous Florida drivers. You still have the same driving skills and quick reflexes you had back when you were cruising around town in your GTO. But be advised that at least half the vehicles with which you will be sharing Florida roads are being driven by people whose radios are tuned to the Sinatra channel on Sirius/XM.

My purpose in writing this chapter is to equip you, if you are thinking about moving here, with vital information you'll need as a Florida driver that will enable you to arrive at your destination with you, your passengers and vehicle intact.

All you have to do is remember two things: A substantial percentage of the elderly drivers you will encounter on your way to the supermarket, golf course or beach can't:

1. See.
2. Hear.

But before I go into specifics, let's get you "on the road," equipped with your very own Florida driver's license.

Getting your license

If you are accustomed to long lines and unfriendly personnel at the DMV in your home state who, when you finally get to the head of the line you have been waiting in for hours, order you to move to another line, here's some good news: Getting your Florida driver's license is a quick and easy process.

Even better news. You needn't study a manual or take a road test conducted by an officer who will make you parallel park or do other impractical things you will never do as a Florida driver.

If you have a driver's license from another state, all that is required to obtain your Florida license is to pass a vision test. This involves looking into a double-barreled microscope, reading the top line of letters on a chart, and identifying a few common road signs you will encounter throughout Florida, such as Yield, Stop and Panther Crossing.

I failed mine. No problem. The clerk allowed me to re-take the test on the spot, showing me the same letters and road signs I had incorrectly identified a moment earlier.

I passed, she congratulated me, and took a picture for my license, which I can renew by mail or online without having to return to the DMV until I am one-hundred years old.

According to Florida DMV guidelines, applicants whose test results indicate they have 20/50 vision or worse in either eye may be referred to a professional for improvement and should submit a Report of Eye Exam to receive their license. (Whether it is necessary to actually *pass* that exam isn't clear. Apparently, all you need is to prove you took it.)

Applicants afflicted with blindness or vision worse than 20/200 in one eye must have at least 20/40 vision in the other eye.

Applicants who, like Orphan Annie, have no eyes, may be required to demonstrate proficiency at reading road signs in Braille.

The last paragraph is made up but the other two aren't. In short, it isn't necessary that you actually have the ability to *see* in order to obtain a Florida driver's license. All you need is to possess a license from another state and the fee.

Now that you have your license, here are five rules for the road every newly-minted Florida driver should know.

Rule #1: Beware of Buicks

Buicks, which nobody under the age of ninety drives in the rest of the country, are extremely popular in Florida — especially in the southwestern part of the state where so many Midwesterners, many of them former Michiganders who once worked for GM, live and vacation.

If you see a Buick nameplate on the back of a car you are following, pull off the highway and give it time to travel at least five miles down the road before resuming your journey.

Don't get me wrong. Buicks are no more dangerous than any other car. But Buick drivers are. Over the last year I have witnessed:

- A Buick Lucerne t-boning a brand-new Jaguar convertible at a busy intersection. The twenty-something Jag driver wept as the elderly Buick driver in stretch pants and a sprayed beehive — not a hair was knocked out of place when her car's airbag deployed — attempted to console her. "Honey, I didn't see you coming."

- A Buick Verano traveling west in the eastbound lane of I-75 across Alligator Alley. Drivers were honking and flashing their lights, trying to alert the white-haired Buick driver to get off the road. He, assuming everyone was being friendly, waved back.

- A collision involving three Buicks – a south-bound Regal that ran a stop light … striking a Lacrosse that was turning left from the north-bound lane … propelling it into a freight car-sized Enclave waiting at the intersection which, in turn, almost ran over me on my bicycle.

Rule # 2: Avoid drivers with "Choose Life" plates

Florida gives car owners more customizable license plate options than any other state — one-hundred forty-seven of them as of January, 2025. Drivers can choose plates announcing their favorite sport, college, animal, team or military branch.

They can even order "Choose Life" plates to encourage pregnant women who don't want the babies they are carrying to give birth to them anyway.

Though they claim to value the sanctity of life, many drivers who display "Choose Life" plates seem to have no regard for the living with whom they share Florida roads.

As a group, Choose Lifers tend to drive slowly, change lanes without warning, sit at green lights until the light turns yellow at which point they make a dash for it, come to sudden stops, and seem unaware of other drivers and pedestrians.

One night in a restaurant parking lot, we saw a Cadillac with "Choose Life" plates back out and strike a young man who was walking behind it, and run over his left leg. The driver, who hadn't heard the victim's screams, continued on his way.

I've petitioned the DMV to offer a "Choose Death" plate but, as of this writing, nobody from Tallahassee has gotten back to me.

Rule #3: Take care in parking lots

Florida parking lots can be particularly hazardous to your health, causing undue exertion that can lead to a heat stroke or heart attack. Up to eighty percent of the spaces in any Florida parking lot are reserved for the handicapped. You can't park in them because you, unlike the drivers of these vehicles, aren't handicapped — you had the foresight to take care of your health. You'll be walking a long way in stifling heat and humidity to any store or doctor's office you want to visit, unless, of course, you obtain a coveted "Handicap" hang tag for your rear-view mirror. You'll be able to use that until your kids take the keys away. (Tip: Borrow a hang-tag from a handicapped friend and take it to Office Depot's Business Center to have it color-copied onto heavyweight photo paper. Cut it out, hang it from your rear-view mirror and you, too, can enjoy priority parking.)

Rule # 4: Keep your brakes in tip-top shape

Everyone in Florida either moved here, or is visiting from, someplace else. Because they're newbies, most drivers have no clue where they are going.

A driver looking for an address with which he is unfamiliar will, likely as not, throw on his brakes and stop at every driveway he comes to in order to check the address on the front of the building or mailbox to see if he's there yet.

Be aware, too, that many elderly Florida drivers inexplicably come to complete stops every time they see a bicyclist — whether the cyclist is ten or even five-hundred feet away. I can understand slowing down to allow extra room between the cyclist and car but why so many drivers come to a dead stop is beyond me — it's as if they saw a space alien and were dumbstruck.

Never tailgate in Florida because, if you do, you'll rear-end one of these brake-happy drivers and the police will say it's your fault. Leave extra space between your car and cars in front of you, check your brake fluid often, and make sure your brake pads are in perfect condition at all times.

Rule #5: Six days of the year to stay off the roads entirely

Hundreds of thousands of snowbirds rent condos for the months of January, February and March. These rentals generally begin on the first and last day of the month.

As a result, I-95 and I-75 are bumper-to-bumper with Buicks headed south on the first day of these months, and north on the last. Stick to side roads on those days.

Follow these tips and you'll arrive at your destination safely.

Better yet, order an Uber.

THE WORST SUPER BOWL
COMMERCIAL EVER

I watched last night's Super Bowl game between the Los Angeles Lakers and Boston Red Sox. I never pay much attention to who's playing. I watch strictly for the commercials which are always more entertaining than the game itself.

As a guy who spent his career creating ads, I was struck by how many of last night's commercials missed the mark completely. The reason? The ad agency folks who created them, and the clients who approved them, forgot to include the unique features and benefits of the products and services they were supposed to be selling.

Many starred celebrities who were paid handsomely to promote themselves, because they sure weren't saying or demonstrating anything about the products they were ostensibly pushing. Disagree? OK then, take this test. What product or service was Kris Jenner promoting? Laura Dern? Dan Levy? Tina Fey? Chris Pratt? Arnold Schwarzenegger? Gimme the name of the brand, not the genre. See what I mean?

But the worst commercial of all didn't feature celebrities. It featured the unhappiest family in America. Here's a recap:

A pre-teen figure skater is performing in a competition.

The camera cuts to her dad in the audience...then back to his daughter as she finishes her routine...raises her arms triumphantly ...

strikes and holds her pose…and flashes a self-conscious but adorable smile.

Cut to the dad. For a split second, he smiles broadly, pleased his daughter did well. But then he glances at the seat beside him, which is empty. He loses his smile, and becomes sad. A singer starts intoning a wrist-slashingly depressing song that continues to the commercial's end. It reminded me of the dirge from the opening scene of *Dr. Zhivago* as young Yuri follows his mother's coffin to her grave.

Cut back to the skater. She is now looking as sad as her dad — she obviously heard the music.

Cut to drone shot of a blue KIA EV9 wending its way along a dark, twisty, snow-covered mountain road.

Cut to the car's interior. Dad is using its navigation system to map out his route.

Cut to the KIA arriving at a remote cabin that, conveniently, has a frozen pond in its yard.

Cut to the cabin's interior where an elderly man — presumably the girl's grandfather — is in a wheelchair.

Cut outside to the girl's dad, who is stringing lights above the pond. He plugs the cord into a socket on his electric car, illuminating the pond.

Cut to the cabin's interior. Someone wheels the old man to the window.

Cut to the pond, where the girl is re-creating her skate show.

Cut back to the old man. He places his hand on his heart and writes "10" (the score an Olympic judge would give for a perfect performance) in the frost on the window with his finger. (I assume he wrote 10 to indicate his approval but perhaps he wrote it to let his son and granddaughter know that's how many days he has left to live since they obviously don't visit often — otherwise they wouldn't have had to use the navigation system to find him.)

Cut to, and hold on, the car parked by the improvised skating rink as announcer intones, "Kia. Movement that Inspires."

I've had bowel movements that inspired me more.

There are so many things wrong with this commercial I hardly know where to begin.

For starters, why did Kia choose a sad situation — a frail, elderly man unable to leave his house? Why, for example, didn't the creators show the girl performing outside a hospital where, from a window, her mother, holding the baby to which she just gave birth, watches her daughter do triple axels and spins? That would have been a happy occasion. Don't you want products that make you feel happy? Of course you do. Everyone does.

Another idea: Everyone these days — even wheelchair-bound old people in mountain cabins — has a smart phone. Why didn't the girl's dad simply take a video of her performance with his phone and text it to the old man?

Why does the music track that plays under the commercial sound like "The Funeral March of a Marionette?" Shouldn't a commercial for a trendy product feature lively and happy music to communicate how using it makes one feel?

Why didn't the girl's dad, when he installed the lights above the frozen pond, simply plug them into an outdoor socket? Wouldn't that have been cheaper, faster and easier than buying an electricity-generating car?

Come to think of it, are there any benefits of owning a Kia EV9 other than being able to use it to generate electricity? Does it reduce CO_2 emissions? If so, that could have been mentioned to appeal to environmentalists. Does it help owners save money on fuel? That benefit would have appealed to budget-conscious viewers. Is it fun to drive? Does it have unique safety features for snowy conditions? How does a Kia EV9 compare to other electric vehicles in its price class? Does it convert, at the touch of a button, into a helicopter? Who the hell would know from this commercial?

Certainly not viewers, though it's a safe bet both the agency and client got VIP tickets to the Super Bowl from CBS which charged something like $15 million to air the spot.

What's the next Kia EV9 commercial going to show? The dad and daughter in their Kia following a hearse carrying the old man's body to the cemetery?

Sure, why not?

SOMEWHERE AT SEA

"The night we met I knew I was going to marry Serena," our ruddy-nosed table companion said, looking lovingly at the tiny woman about my age seated between us as she guzzled her third flute of Champagne in the ten minutes since we had been shown to their table. "But I wasn't looking forward to going home and telling my wife."

My wife and I are on day five of a twelve-day cruise from Lisbon to Florida. Some of our friends think we're crazy — they say they would lose their minds being confined to a ship that long — but on previous cruises, we've found we actually prefer the days "at sea" so here we are aboard the Azamara Onward. The Onward is smaller than most cruise ships — just six hundred guests.

We're having a swell time. Literally. The weather was perfect for the first four days but last night around dinnertime we entered choppy seas with swells of up to fifteen feet, which are supposed to continue until tomorrow. Sunday morning we'll dock in Bermuda for two days, then continue on to Ft. Lauderdale, arriving a week from today.

The food is excellent and available around the clock. I woke up hungry at 2 a.m. the first night out — I was still on Florida time — and considered taking advantage of the twenty-four-hour room service but didn't want to wake my wife.

There are, if we choose to avail ourselves of them, nonstop activities — multiple trivia games, daily "Name That Tune" competitions in the lounge during tea, bridge games, lectures, classes, bingo, mahjong, virtual golf, dance lessons and more. There is a nicely-equipped fitness center, a spa and a walking track around the top deck and, at night, entertainment in the lounge. Sometimes the ship's entertainment staff puts on a show. Other nights feature professional singers, musicians, comedians or magicians, most of whom earn their livelihoods performing on cruise ships like this. As much as we enjoy cruising, I can't even imagine having to live on a ship.

Hands-down, the most entertaining part of this cruise, as is the case on every cruise we've taken — we aren't sure if this is our seventh or eighth but it is most definitely the longest — is talking with our fellow passengers including:

- The fashionably dressed seventy-ish woman from New Zealand who presides, from just after breakfast until at least 10 p.m. when the stage show ends, over the smoking section on deck nine near the pool where, every fifteen minutes or so, an attendant, without asking, brings her a cold bottle of Stella Artois. She says this is the tenth time she has taken this particular transatlantic cruise. Amazingly, she seems as coherent at night as she was in the morning. All the crew members seem to know her. Why she feels compelled to spend money on cruises when she could stay home in New Zealand and drink and smoke herself to death is beyond me, but she is an endless source of information about the crew and who's doing what with whom.
- A dapper Scotsman who looks to be in his early eighties and his gorgeous blonde twenty-something daughter. That's the relationship we assumed when we met them at the port in

Lisbon while waiting to board, but turns out they're married. She's his fourth wife — his first ended in divorce, his next two wives died, and they've been married for five years. Whenever the orchestra plays, they're on the dance floor, their hands all over each other. They asked us to join their trivia team and both are wicked-smart. He is a retired physician; she's a veterinarian but doesn't practice because, like so many people aboard this ship, they spend four or five months of the year taking cruises. Good for them.

- The female half of a couple we met at bridge who said she owes her life to Evita Peron. Her parents, who fled the Nazis, had settled in Peru where, in the late 1940s, the medical facilities were primitive. A Peruvian doctor told her pregnant mother he could either save her life but her baby would die, or vice versa, but no way he could save both. Our friend's grandmother, who had moved to Argentina, sent a letter to Evita, wife of the country's president, begging her to arrange for her daughter to have the baby in an Argentine hospital where both would have better chances of survival. Evita took care of everything, and both the mother and baby, our new friend, survived. Today, oddly enough, we attended a lecture on Broadway musicals of the 1970s and the presenter described *Evita* as the story of a despicable woman. Our new friend didn't attend but she could have set him straight.

Last night we were seated at a table with two other couples, including the aforementioned Robert and Serena. Before she became incoherent, Serena told me they spend four or five months a year cruising. They have earned diamond status in several cruise lines' loyalty programs (excuse me, programmes, they're Canadian) which means they can book a regular cabin and, if one is available, get upgraded to a suite. Serena, we couldn't help but note, clearly loves to drink. So does Robert but he holds his liquor better. Perhaps that's why they are loyal to Azamara — the drinks are included in the fare. They have been together for forty-seven years.

Robert said he was married with three children the night he met Serena. He went home and told his wife he was leaving her for his new love. The divorce was ugly and protracted. A few months after it was finalized, his ex-wife married his stepfather. And when Robert's stepfather and his new wife, who was now Robert's step mother-in-law in addition to being his ex, had children of their own, their new children became not only Robert's children's half-siblings but their half-uncles and -aunts.

"When my kids had to draw their family trees in school, it was really fucked up," he said.

Serena, as this story was unfolding, switched to Chardonnay and finally told the waiter to leave the bottle on the table. That is against the cruise line's policy but, since he was having to refill her glass every two minutes, he didn't object. By the time dessert arrived, she had ordered two glasses of port. When we saw them at the stage show after dinner, she had returned to Champagne.

At lunch today we ran into the other couple who had been at our table. They told us that, after the stage show, Serena had tumbled down the grand staircase between the fifth floor and lobby, and had to be taken to the infirmary where it was discovered she had no broken bones, just a few bumps, bruises and scratches. Amazing.

Serena and Robert hurried past and waved at us with their free hands. His other hand was holding a glass of red wine, hers held a tall glass with a wedge of pineapple and a cute little tropical umbrella on top. We laughed and joked that perhaps they were going to the Friends of Bill W meeting — cruise lines always list a "Bill W" meeting on the daily schedule rather than call it what it actually is, an "AA" meeting — but we somehow doubted it.

When we saw Robert and Serena later, they said they had been at a Blind Wine Tasting event. It was a lot of fun and it's too bad we hadn't joined them.

A week to go. More people to meet. More stories. We're having fun, and looking forward to our first Thanksgiving dinner at sea. Tonight's stage show is a performance by an Irish magician. At his first show three nights ago, he picked me out of the audience to be his on-stage assistant and the butt of his jokes, but I didn't mind.

This time we'll know better than to sit in the front row.

HIGH IN THE LOW SEVENTIES

During my college years, my mother fretted I would turn into one of those pot-smoking hippies she saw on TV. A liberal when it came to most social issues, she was anything but liberal about drugs and did everything she could to dissuade me, her baby, from using them.

She even suggested the campus police shouldn't give students arrested for pot the benefit of due process. She said the offenders should be strung up, without a trial, from the six free-standing columns in the middle of the quadrangle, the only remnants of a building that had burned to the ground in the 1890s, and left to rot. That, she said, would remind me not to smoke pot.

I pointed out that my fellow students might have trouble concentrating on their studies if, as they hurried to class, they had to pass their classmates' putrid carcasses dangling in the breeze, being picked apart by buzzards.

I'm not going to pretend I didn't smoke weed during my college years — I don't know anyone who didn't — but mom needn't have worried. I wasn't a pothead but some of my friends were. A few, fifty-some years later, still are. One claims he has smoked a joint every day for fifty-five years with no adverse effects — something his four ex-wives and dozens of former employers might dispute.

After graduation, I continued to, on occasion, indulge. Weed was readily accessible in the advertising business — as easy to buy as sketch pads and typewriter ribbons. I stopped pretty much for good when we had our first kid although, if someone offered me a joint, I gladly accepted. Just one toke. Maybe two. (Note to my children and grandchildren: Your mother and grandmother never, not once, smoked pot. But she, as you know, does like her Sauvignon Blanc.)

For years I told people that, when I retired, I planned to smoke weed every day provided I could find a reliable source. And why not? Almost everyone my age drinks, but I've never been a big drinker. Two cocktails and I'm three sheets to the wind. Three drinks and I projectile vomit. Once retired, I wouldn't have to drive or deliver coherent work, and would have endless days to languish by my pool stoned out of my mind. But I wasn't really serious and didn't do anything about finding a source. Until two years ago when my wife and I went to dinner at another couple's house.

After dinner, the host, a fellow retired creative type, asked, "Want some marijuana?"

"Sure!" I replied.

He brought out a bag packed with every conceivable form of pot I had ever heard of, plus some I hadn't — pre-rolled joints packed as tightly and uniformly as cigarettes, capsules, candies, cookies, vape pens, creams, and pills.

"Where did you get all this?"

"I have a medical marijuana prescription."

"How'd you get it?"

"It's easy. You go to one of the storefront marijuana clinics, meet with a doctor, tell him what's wrong with you, hand over a hundred eighty-nine dollars, and walk out with a prescription good for six months. Then you go to a dispensary and buy whatever you want."

"Do you have a medical condition you need it for?"

"I told the doctor I have back pain."

"Do you?"

"No."

"I was under the impression you had to be in the final stages of a terminal disease to get a medical pot prescription. Do you think I can get one?"

"Sure."

"What should I tell the doctor?"

"Tell him anything — hell, tell him you have a wart on your dick — and you'll walk out with a prescription and an official card issued by the state of Florida you can use to buy anything you want. Pot docs have an incentive to say yes; they don't get paid otherwise."

The next morning I drove to a Medical Marijuana clinic in a nearby strip mall. The waiting room was packed. Old folks, some older than me. A businessman in a suit. A couple wearing Burger King uniforms. A woman in tennis attire. A construction worker. None looked the least bit sick. Every few minutes the front desk attendant called out a name. The patient walked down the hall and returned to the lobby quickly, looking pleased.

As I was awaiting my turn, the attendant said I could save time by paying the fee before I saw the doctor. I said I'd rather pay it once I had my prescription in hand. He laughed. "You don't have anything to worry about, you'll get it." I handed over my credit card. He processed my payment and led me down the hall into a windowless room where a doctor was seated behind a card table.

"What are you here for?" the doctor, a disheveled thirty-something wearing a sweatshirt with the name of a Caribbean medical school, asked. I had prepared my spiel and it was true: "I have tinnitus (ringing in the ears). It's annoying and my doctor says there's nothing he can do to relieve it."

He typed a prescription into his computer and sent it to the State Department of Health in Tallahassee. "Pick up your temporary card at the front desk and you can go to a dispensary today. Here's a coupon for fifty dollars off if you spend a hundred dollars or more. Your permanent card will come in the mail in a couple of weeks."

A few minutes later I walked into a dispensary — there were six to choose from within two miles of the clinic with names like Jungle Boys and Cookies — presented my card, and was escorted into a dimly-lit back room by an "advisor" sporting a nose ring, silver dollar-sized ear gauges, and a sleeve of tattoos. Glass-fronted cases of marijuana in multiple forms were as artfully and carefully arranged as diamonds in a jewelry store.

I told him I wanted something to help me forget my tinnitus. The guy seemed chill, so I also told him something I hadn't mentioned to the doctor — I wanted weed that would make me as euphoric as the pot I used to smoke in my younger days.

He explained there are three types of medical marijuana. Indica is for relaxation and calmness. That's what I needed to alleviate the tinnitus. Sativa energizes, uplifts and stimulates creativity, the perfect prescription for euphoria. Hybrid is a combination of both.

My wife rolled her eyes when I came home carrying a bag containing two-hundred dollars' worth of pot for which I had paid one-hundred fifty with my discount coupon. I had signed up for the dispensary's "High Times" frequent buyers' club to earn points for future savings. I promised her I'd never use it during the daytime or if knew I'd be driving — only after dinner when we watch TV. No woman wants to live with a young man who's stoned all day much less an old one.

Over the next few months I worked my way through the bag's contents. The smokable pot made me cough uncontrollably. I couldn't keep the smoke in my lungs long enough for it to take effect. The vape pen did, too. The gummies did nothing for me — I might as well have been eating Swedish goldfish — nor did the cookies or lollipops. The lotion, which the advisor promised would relieve sore muscles, also did nothing and, within a few days after I opened the jar, became rock-hard, rendering it unusable. I threw most of it away.

When I went back to the store and told my advisor I was disappointed, he recommended a bottle of Sativa in tincture form — bottled marijuana oil suspended in a solution users draw into a medicine dropper then swallow.

Ka-ching. The tincture worked like a charm. It made everything more vivid, more intense. I didn't just watch TV shows. I became a participant in them.

But there was one problem. Within a half-hour, I fell into a deep sleep on the sofa. And when my wife shook me awake so I would come to bed, my dreams were bizarre. One night I dreamed I had just been named Biden's press secretary, and was panicking because I was standing in front of the podium and nobody had told me what to say.

For months I experimented to find the dose that would produce the perfect high I had enjoyed in my younger days without knocking me out but I never found it.

And while I returned to the doctor to renew my prescription several times, and visited other dispensaries to try new brands and delivery mechanisms, it all, after a while, became boring. And stupid. Not to mention expensive.

In November, 2024, Florida voters were asked if they wanted to allow dispensaries to sell pot for recreational purposes. Approval would put marijuana doctors out of business, enabling dispensaries to dispense with the pretense of providing health services and sell legal weed to anyone twenty-one and over. My prescription had expired a few months before the election. I had decided to wait for the recreational initiative to pass, so I wouldn't have to shell out another one-hundred eighty-nine dollars to renew it. Donald Trump appeared in ads urging Floridians to vote yes. So did John Morgan, the billionaire founder of America's largest personal injury law firm. Governor Ron DeSantis, a straight arrow, opposed it. To my surprise, Floridians rejected the measure.

A few nights ago, I used my last drops of tincture and decided that's it. While I enjoyed the highs, at my age I need to stay awake. I've lost friends who, without warning, slipped into permanent sleep. There's so much I still want to do. I want to write more. There are books I've been meaning to read, places I haven't seen, and other places I want to revisit. I can't do any of those things if I'm asleep because I was seeking to recapture the euphoria of my youth which, I should have been smart enough to realize, is gone forever.

My marijuana days are behind me unless, of course, I come down with some fatal disease in which case I'll return to the doctor for a new prescription.

Until then, I'm clean.

BARGAIN TO THE MAXX

TD: So what's in the TJ Maxx bag?

JD: You know I love the Movado watch you gave me. I wear it all the time. Don't be insulted but…I bought another one. *(Opens box to reveal it.)*

TD: Nice!

JD: This one's completely different. It's gold. The one you gave me is stainless steel. Do you like it?

TD: Sure, it's great. Why would I get mad?

JD: Well, see the price on the box?

TD: Five hundred-fifty dollars. Wow.

JD: OK, that's the retail price. Look at this tag with TJ's price: Two twenty-nine ninety-nine.

TD: Almost half-off. Good for you.

JD: But, it was clearance priced. Just one eighty-nine.

TD: Another forty dollars off. Not bad!

JD: I'm just getting started. Today was Senior Day – ten percent off everything in the store for people fifty-five and older. That saved another eighteen dollars and ninety cents.

TD: So now we're down to, what, a hundred-seventy or so?

JD: Yeah, but they added sales tax so as you can see here on the receipt — a total of one hundred-eighty dollars and thirty-one cents.

TD: Not too shabby!

JD: I had a hundred-dollar gift card from my birthday, so that made it eighty.

TD: Damn, that's impressive!

JD: Plus, my account had a twenty-six-dollar forty-nine cent credit from something I returned a year ago.

TD: OK, you're at, like, fifty-four bucks here.

JD: Plus, for every two-hundred dollars I spend, I get a ten-dollar credit certificate and I had five of those I was worried were gonna expire so I applied them. Look at this *(indicating amount on receipt)*. I got a five hundred-fifty-dollar Movado watch for a grand total of three dollars and eighty-two cents. People around me at checkout were applauding. The cashier said I win the prize for the bargain of the week.

TD: I'll admit it, that's pretty good.

JD: Yeah. You're sure you're not upset? I really do love the one you got me.

TD: No problem. I didn't know you needed another watch.

JD: I don't.

DEATH AND TAXES

Monday April 20, 2015

I am headed to Missouri, behind the wheel of a red Avis Lincoln. Thursday morning, my mother is having elective surgery that, if she weren't 102, would be considered routine. The doctor assures us her odds are excellent but I want to be there anyway.

I'm driving rather than flying because — this may sound strange — I want to go through Alabama, the only state east of the Mississippi I've never been to. I will drop the rental car off at the St. Louis airport and fly home a week from today.

I had originally planned to leave early this morning which would put me in Missouri tomorrow night, but came down with the flu Friday. I was worried I would still be contagious if I got there tomorrow — I don't want to infect mom. From what I've been able to learn online, there's no likelihood of contagion if I arrive Wednesday, a day later than planned.

Thirty miles east of Tallahassee, I call home. My wife says a letter from the IRS has arrived and asks if I want her to open it.

"Sure," I tell her.

She opens it and immediately becomes hysterical. "It says we owe four-million two-hundred thousand five-hundred five dollars and seventy cents ($4,200,505.70) by April 30."

"What?"

"What have you done?" she demands.

"I have no idea what this is about," I reply.

I ask her to read it to me. She does. I ask her to read it again.

The letter, from the IRS' Cincinnati office, is addressed to the Dryden Partners 401K Plan. I closed my agency in 2011 but haven't yet rolled the assets of the one employee who remains invested in the plan — me — into an IRA. There's no rush. Last summer, for the first time, I took money from the plan. We had to close on a house we purchased before we received the proceeds of one we sold, and needed the cash. I owed $36,000 in taxes on the withdrawal. All the details — the withdrawal and tax payment — were handled by the Connecticut benefits company that, for twenty years, has administered the plan.

I had hoped to make Alabama tonight but not now. "I'm going to turn around. I'll be home around midnight," I tell my wife.

"No," she reminds me. "Your mom is counting on you."

"OK then, take pictures of all the pages and text them to me. I'm going to check in to the first hotel I come to."

Thirty minutes later I'm in the room of a Holiday Inn Express, re-reading the letter for the fifth time. It says I owe $3,600,000 plus penalties, interest and failure-to-file fees — a grand total of $4,200,505.70. I email it to Mary, my long-time advisor at the Connecticut benefits company and ask her to call me first thing in the morning.

I sleep, at most, an hour. My stomach bug has returned.

Tuesday, April 21

I have already stopped at two gas stations to use the facilities when, somewhere in southwestern Georgia, I receive an email from Mary. She says it appears an IRS computer has mistakenly added two zeroes to the

$36,000 I paid, and somehow came to the bizarre conclusion I owe $3.6 million plus interest and penalties. "This should be easy to resolve but we need you to sign a Power of Attorney giving us the right to speak to the IRS on your behalf. I'm going to email it to you and I need your real signature, not an e-signature, so you'll have to print it out, sign it, and fax it back.

I call her. "I don't have any way to print it out. I'm driving through Georgia. I'm sick to my stomach. I haven't slept. Can't you just call them without my signature?"

"No," she replies firmly. "We're dealing with the IRS here."

"OK, I'll find a place where I can print it out, sign it, and fax it back to you."

In Podunk, Alabama, I stop at a pack and ship store that has a neon "Fax" sign in the window. The clerk explains his fax works fine but his printer is broken. Shit.

Two hours later, I stop at the business center of an office superstore in a Birmingham suburb. Its printer is broken, too. "You have a hundred printers on your shelves, take one out of a box," I plead. "We can't do that," the clerk explains.

I throw up in the parking lot. My khakis, from the knees down, are covered with puke. I clean myself up the best I can and email Mary to tell her I'll send it from the casino hotel I'm planning to stay in tonight in Tunica, Mississippi. I'd hoped to have a little fun along the way. Silly me.

Shortly before sundown, I walk into the lobby of my hotel. It looks elegant. Its patrons don't — big-bellied good ole boys, some wearing bib overalls, and blue-haired women in polyester stretch pants. Even in my vomit-stained slacks, I'm probably the best-dressed person in the joint. I head to the concierge desk. The man sitting behind it informs me he's not the concierge, the concierge only works on weekends.

I ask where the business center is, explaining I have a document I need to print out, sign and fax. "It ain't open, it closed at five." he says. He tells me to inquire at the front desk.

The desk clerk says the manager will be able to accommodate me. She has a printer and fax in her office, but she's not around — she should be back momentarily.

"I'm going to my room to change clothes. Please call the minute she returns," I tell her. "It's important."

An hour later, having received no call, I'm back at the front desk. "Oh, there she is," the clerk announces, indicating a woman shuffling across the lobby.

Ten minutes later, I've printed out and signed the POA form and given the clerk the fax number of the benefits company. "I want a printout confirming it went through," I tell her, handing her the form and cover sheet. "No problem," she smiles as she disappears into the manager's office.

She returns, bringing the original document and a sheet of paper confirming it was received at the other end. I slip her a twenty-dollar bill, and return to my room. I am sick all night, but at least I sleep some. My stomach, by now, is empty; there's nothing in it to expel.

Wednesday, April 22

As I'm crossing into Missouri around 11 a.m., I get a text from Mary. She says she received two blank pages. The idiot clerk in Mississippi faxed the POA and cover sheet upside-down. "We can't call the IRS until we have it."

I stop at the Missouri Welcome Center. "Do you have a fax?" I ask the greeter. "Yes, but we can't let you use it." "Please," I beseech her. "I'm desperate here." She says there's a truck stop fifty miles up the road in Hayti that has a public fax machine.

I hightail it up I-55. An hour later, the signed POA is in Mary's hands. I know for sure because I call her to confirm it. Someone from the benefits company can now call the IRS and straighten this out.

I stop at a Dairy Queen and order a Blizzard, the first food I've had since I left home two days ago.

My mother is asleep when I arrive at her assisted living apartment in Columbia around 4 p.m. Checking email, I'm relieved to see Mary has written that her office spoke with the IRS and pointed out the mistake which they seem to understand. She says the IRS has promised I'll get a letter within thirty to forty-five days acknowledging the mix-up and assures me they no longer expect me to pay the $4.2 million and change by the end of the month.

Thursday, April 23

At 6 a.m. I take mom to the hospital where we are met by my sister and nephew. They live in Missouri. They could have taken her but I volunteered to — too much of mom's care has fallen on their shoulders over the years. I am retired, have the free time, and want to be there as much for them as for mom.

By 10 a.m. mom is in the recovery room. She says she was conscious the whole time and watched her angioplasty procedure on the video monitor. She says it was fascinating. The doctor says she did great, but he'll keep her in the hospital overnight.

My sister and her son depart. She is going to her home on the other side of town. My nephew is headed back to his office near Kansas City.

Around 3 p.m., as mom is napping, I call my sister to report our mother is doing fine. She warns me not to get upset but she is in the town's other hospital. She is having symptoms of a heart attack. I rush there, sit with her a while in the E.R. and call her son to let him know what is happening.

I hurry back to mom's bedside. She asks where I've been. "I took a long walk," I lie.

When I leave at 7:30, mom is watching Martha Stewart on TV. "She looks like she's had some work," mom says, commenting on Martha's unnaturally unlined face. I kiss the top of her head and rush across town to the hospital where my sister is being kept overnight and stay with her until 9.

Friday, April 24
First thing, I call my sister from her condo where I spent the night. She says it wasn't a heart attack, it was stress, the doctors are being overly cautious. She expects to be dismissed around noon. So I head to mom's hospital.

When I walk into her room it is clear something has gone terribly wrong. Mom is in her bed, which has been cranked up to a sitting position, a breakfast tray in front of her. She looks at me but there's no recognition in her eyes, no expression on her face. She isn't moving, her food is untouched. She is silent -- no "Good morning" or "How did you sleep?" from her. Why the hell haven't any of nurses, yakking at their station outside mom's room, noticed? I ask one what happened. She says mom's chart indicates she cried out in the middle of the night and the nurse on duty gave her a shot of morphine. The nurse says the morphine probably made her groggy and reminds me mom is, after all, 102 years old.

Mom's condition deteriorates as the morning progresses. Her eyes are open but she can't speak, her blood pressure is headed south. She begins drifting in and out of consciousness. Mid-morning a nurse comes in and cheerfully announces that mom has to vacate her room by noon. I ask, "Where do you expect me to take her? She's comatose." The nurse says it's hospital policy — otherwise we will be charged for another day. I demand to speak with a patient advocate. The moment the advocate sees mom, she agrees. Mom's staying.

I go down to the lobby to call my brother in Ohio. He was delighted when I reported yesterday that mom had come through her procedure with flying colors. I tell him things have taken a turn for the worse.

When I return to mom's room, there's a crash cart outside the door. The advocate called mom's doctor, and he has brought other doctors with him. He asks me to sign a form allowing him to give mom a blood transfusion. I tell him I don't have the authority to make mom's medical decisions – only my sister does. At that moment my sister walks into the room, wearing a white dress. An angel. She signs the form.

Mom receives multiple transfusions that afternoon. Her blood pressure continues to drop. Every so often she vomits black bile.

My nephew and his fiancé arrive late in the afternoon.

At 7 p.m. I'm outside the hospital's entrance, smoking a cigarette and talking with my wife. "I don't think I can handle much more of this," I tell her.

"Well, try to relax," she says. We laugh.

My sister and I leave the hospital around 10 p.m. and go to her condo. My nephew and his fiancé are spending the night keeping vigil in mom's room.

Saturday, April 25

Mom dies at 7 a.m., as my sister and I are entering the hospital's lobby.

Sunday April 26

I call the airline to cancel my reservation for tomorrow's flight home and rebook it for Thursday. I call Avis and extend the car rental four days.

Monday, April 27 – Wednesday, April 29

The next three days are a blur of burial arrangements, cleaning out mom's apartment, going through her things, making plans for the memorial service. My brother and sister-in-law have arrived. Yes, mom was 102 but we're all in shock. We didn't expect this. We thought she was immortal.

Thursday, April 30

I drive 120 miles to the St. Louis airport and drop off the car at the Avis lot. The check-in agent says he can't give me a receipt, his printer is broken — a theme I've heard often over the last few days. He says he will email it to me.

Back in Florida that night, as I am about to turn in, I check my email. No receipt. I go online to avis.com. There's no receipt because there's no record I returned the car. It occurs to me I may have been scammed. Perhaps the reason the agent couldn't give me a receipt is that he wasn't an Avis employee in the first place so he couldn't produce one. Maybe he was an impostor in an Avis uniform who took the keys and drove the car off the lot. It's probably in a chop shop somewhere and I'm on the hook for $50,000 or whatever a Lincoln costs.

I call Avis' 800 number. It's impossible to reach a human. I hang up and call a special number reserved for elite renters like I used to be but no longer am. The agent laughs — actually *laughs* — when I explain my concern. For thirteen years Avis was my client and we signed off every ad, brochure and direct mail piece with the company's longtime slogan, "We try harder." A more fitting slogan would be, "We don't try at all."

The agent says I have to call the St. Louis Avis office and gives me the number. I try for an hour but nobody picks up. I call the elite renter number again. A different agent gives me the manager's number in St. Louis. I leave a message on her machine and wait an hour but she doesn't call back. I try the office number again. This time I reach someone who assures me things like this happen all the time and he will go out in the lot, look for the car and, *if it's there*, will close out my contract and email the receipt.

"Do it now," I beg. He says he will.

An hour later, having received nothing, I go to bed but toss and turn all night.

Monday, May 1

Checking email, the receipt has arrived. The car was in the lot after all. At least one thing has broken my way this week.

Saturday, May 23

Today's mail contains the long-awaited letter from the IRS in Cincinnati. I no longer owe them $4,200,505.70. The new total is $4,368,312.11, payable by June 5. They've added $167,806.41 in penalties and interest since last month.

It's the first day of the three-day Memorial Day weekend. The benefits company is closed. So is the IRS. There's nobody to talk to, nothing I can do but stew for the next three days and imagine IRS agents seizing my bank accounts and our house and cars and dogs before hauling me off to jail, all because I didn't pay millions I never owed in the first place.

Tuesday, May 26

I send the letter to Mary at the benefits company then call her. She reiterates her office talked to the IRS on April 22, and was assured the matter was taken care of. She says she will call again and asks me to be available so she can patch me in on the call. I stay home all day waiting for a call that doesn't come.

Wednesday, May 27

Mary calls. She had a family emergency and apologizes for not getting back to me. She spoke to the IRS. The agent she spoke with told her he understands what happened. I've heard that before.

Thursday, May 28

A letter arrives from the IRS. This one is from their office in Ogden, Utah. It thanks me for my "inquiry of April 22" and says they have "corrected your account based on the information you provided." It is a form letter that concludes, "We apologize for any inconvenience."

HOW OLD WOULD
HONEY BEE?

I'm driving down U.S. 41, listening to an oldies station, when Bobby Goldsboro's "Honey," a 1968 chart-topper in which a sadist relates the horrific tale of his dysfunctional marriage and his wife's tragic death, starts playing.

Here's the synopsis: Cruel husband laughs at wife, "Honey," for planting a twig in the yard. He laughs again when she slips and almost splits her head open while running out to brush snow from the twig, which has miraculously taken root. Referring to her as simple-minded ("kinda dumb and kinda smart"), he buys Honey a puppy, then complains when the dog keeps him awake on Christmas Eve. Not surprisingly, he often finds Honey crying "needlessly." She says she's crying because of some sappy TV movie but anyone can see it's because she's trapped in an abusive relationship. She wrecks the car (probably while trying to escape) and is terrified he will erupt but, uncharacteristically, he lets it go. (Poor Honey never knows from one day to the next how the monster she married will react.) One day he comes home "unexpectedly" and finds her weeping yet again but Honey has a good reason. She's dying. He makes no effort to comfort her.

Now, here comes the most disturbing part:

"One day when I was not at home,
When she was there and all alone,
The angels came.
Now all I have is (sic) memories ...."

Where to begin?

For starters, why did she die alone? Why wasn't Honey in a hospital or hospice?

Why would anyone leave a terminal patient at home by herself and go out? Where did he go? To CVS for drugs to relieve her suffering? To the corner bar to watch a game with his buddies? To a Nixon campaign rally? (Remember, this was 1968.) To work? Surely his employer would have understood if he called and said, "I'm not coming in today. Honey's dying."

If he had to be gone, why didn't he at least call someone to hold her hand as she slipped away — a nurse or minister perhaps? Why not call Honey's family? Had he cut her off from all contact? I can't imagine her parents or siblings wouldn't have come if they knew how sick she was.

Who, exactly, was Goldsboro referring to when he sang, "the angels came?" The Visiting Angels whose TV commercials claim they provide affordable in-home health care? The Guardian Angels who patrol New York subways? The California Angels infield? The Hells Angels, bringing chains to beat her and put her out of her misery quickly?

And what did he do when he arrived home and found "the angels came?" Cradle her lifeless body in his arms and weep? Call 9-1-1? Plop down in front of the TV to watch *Gomer Pyle USMC*? Maybe she wasn't dead yet — he's not a doctor, he's a performer — and could have been saved. He doesn't think it's important enough to tell us.

What's more disturbing than the song itself is why, nearly sixty years ago when it was released, people didn't demand that Goldsboro be jailed for spousal abuse. Instead, they went out and bought the record, making him rich, which encouraged him to record another chart-topping maudlin song about a marriage that ended with the unexplained death of a spouse, "The Autumn of My Life."

Realistically, I guess people didn't know better back then. Men were the head of their households and wives of men like Goldsboro were expected to suffer in silence. There were no TV psychologists, books or podcasts telling them how to get out of abusive relationships.

It's a shame, a crying shame, because Honey might be alive today had she lived in more enlightened times. She could have divorced the bastard, married someone who didn't treat her like shit, had children, retired to Florida, and Goldsboro would almost certainly have died in jail where he belonged.

HAM I AM

Where: The deli counter of my local Publix Supermarket.
When: 5:30 p.m., the busiest time of day. A dozen or so shoppers are milling about, numbered tickets in hand, waiting to be served.
Cast of characters: A thirty-ish male clerk wearing a hairnet working behind the counter, an eighty-ish woman and — in two brief guest appearances — me.
Clerk (*standing behind the counter, speaking loudly as he looks around trying to identify the next customer*)**:** Number thirty-two. Number thirty-two. Thirty-two anyone? OK then, thirty-three.
TD: That's me. I'd like a …
Woman (*holding her ticket up and regarding me accusingly as if she has caught me lifting her wallet from her purse*)**:** Wait a minute, I was here first! I'm thirty-two.
Clerk (*turning from me and toward her*)**:** Sorry about that. How can I help you today?
Woman: I want some ham.
Clerk: Boar's Head or Publix?
Woman: What's the difference?
Clerk: We sell a lot of both, but Boar's Head costs more. It's worth it.

Woman: I wouldn't know, I don't generally order lunch meat. It's disgusting what they put in it. Boar's Head, I guess. I'm making sandwiches for my Mexican train group.

Clerk: What kind of ham would you like?

Woman: What are my choices?

Clerk *(leaning down behind the counter and opening the glass door to read the labels)*: Let's see, we have Deluxe … Black Forest … Tavern … Maple Glazed … Pepper … Pesto Parmesan … Low Sodium … and Rosemary and Sundried Tomato.

Woman: Would you repeat that? I can't hear you when you're hiding behind the case mumbling like that.

Clerk *(standing up and gesturing toward the hams in the glass case)*: There are signs in front of each type.

Woman *(Thirty seconds later after she has carefully examined the signs)*: Pesto Parmesan. That sounds interesting.

Clerk: Would you like to try a slice?

Woman: Sure.

(He removes the block of ham, takes it to the back counter, unwraps it, places it on the slicer, and shaves off a slice, which he places on a piece of cello wrap and hands to her. She looks at it closely, sniffs it, then crinkles her nose.)

Woman: What's that green stuff?

Clerk: Pesto.

Woman: What's pesto?

Clerk: It's Italian — garlic, basil, olive oil and, if I remember correctly, ground up pine nuts. It's pretty good over pasta.

Woman: Garlic? I hate garlic!

(She thrusts the slice back toward him as if it's a live hand grenade.)

Clerk: OK then, do you see anything else you might like?

Woman *(after again examining the ham varieties closely)*: Black Forest.

Clerk: Excellent choice, my personal favorite.

Woman: I bet you have to carry that because of all the Germans who winter here, right?

Clerk: I can't answer that ma'am, but it is popular with our German customers.

Woman: Are you German?

Clerk: No, my family's Italian.

Woman: No wonder you recommended that — what was it you called it? — Presto. The one with all that garlic.

Clerk: Would you like to try a slice of Black Forest?

Woman: No. My next-door neighbors are from Dusseldorf. It might be Stuttgart. I'm not sure. I wouldn't like German ham, it would remind me of them. They flew home yesterday and I'm not going to miss their comings and goings for one minute, believe you me!

Clerk: You probably want the Deluxe Ham then — a traditional ham, nothing added to it.

Woman: Let me try that.

Clerk: Of course.

(He repeats the process he had followed with the first sample and hands a slice to her on a piece of cello wrap.)

Woman *(after tasting it)*: Yes, that's what I had in mind. How much is that?

Clerk: It's fourteen-dollars sixty-nine cents a pound.

Woman *(taking a step backward and pointing to the hams in the case)*: Well! That costs the same as the other, fancier hams! Why are you charging just as much if it's easier to make?

Clerk: I don't set the prices ma'am, but it's our most popular ham.

Woman: That doesn't seem right.

Clerk: The Tavern ham is on special this week — twelve ninety-nine a pound.

Woman: I don't drink, so I don't want Tavern ham.

Clerk: There's no alcohol in it.

Woman: Then why do they call it Tavern ham?

Clerk: I wouldn't know. Would you like a sample slice?

Woman: Of course, I'm not going to serve my guests something I haven't tried myself.

(He goes through the sampling ritual again and hands her a slice, which she eats slowly.)

Woman *(reluctantly)***:** I guess that'll do.

Clerk: Great! How much do you want?

Woman: Four slices.

Clerk: You want four *slices* of Tavern ham?

She: Isn't that what I just said?

Clerk: OK, coming right up.

(He takes the ham from case, carries it to the counter, removes the cello wrap and places it on the slicer. He slices one piece, and presents it to her.) Is that about right?

Woman (waving her hand dismissively): No. Thinner.

Clerk: All righty then, thinner it is. *(He adjusts the slicer and shaves off another slice he holds up for her approval.)* How's that?

Woman: Fine.

(He slices three more, places them in a plastic bag, weighs it, slaps a price sticker on it, places it atop the counter and pushes it toward her.)

Clerk: There you go, have a nice day. *(Turning to me.)* Sorry for the wait. How can I help you?

Me: I'd like …

She: Just a minute. I want some cheese.

HEARING THINGS

Lab assistant *(reviewing a checklist at radiology center where I am about to have CAT scan)*: Do you have a pacemaker?
TD: No.
Lab assistant: Any other electronic implants or devices?
TD: No.
Lab assistant: Stents?
TD: No.
Lab assistant: Shunts?
TD: No.
Lab assistant: Body piercings?
TD: Nope.
Lab assistant: Hand grenades?
TD: *Hand grenades?* Do I look like a terrorist? I'm a grandfather! I have white hair! I was Missouri State President of Children of the American Revolution for Chrissakes!
Lab assistant: Sir, I said, "hearing aids."
TD: Oh. I'm sorry I raised my voice. Yes, I do…but I'm not wearing them.
Lab assistant: Obviously.

10 THINGS I MISS MOST
ABOUT CONNECTICUT

Almost thirty years to the day after we moved to Connecticut, we sold our Wilton house and moved to Florida.

We bought our first Florida vacation home in 2003, and have owned two more since then, so it's not like we're going to have trouble acclimating — we already know our way around. Nevertheless, there are things I'm going to miss about the state in which we raised two sons, five dogs and two turtles. Here are the top ten:

> **1. Autumn:** Fall in New England is a kaleidoscope of colors
> — reds, yellows, browns and oranges.
> **2. Lying in bed, hearing the whistle of the last Metro North passenger train of the night as it approached a crossing a mile away:** It always reminded me of a poem by Edna St. Vincent Millay.

The railroad track is miles away,
And the day is loud with voices speaking,
Yet there isn't a train goes by all day
But I hear its whistle shrieking.

All night there isn't a train goes by,
Though the night is still for sleep and dreaming,
But I see its cinders red on the sky,
And hear its engine steaming.

My heart is warm with the friends I make,
And better friends I'll not be knowing:
Yet there isn't a train I wouldn't take,
No matter where it's going.

3. The Wilton Public Library: It stocked the latest nonfiction releases. The library here in Bonita Springs doesn't. Floridians are too busy with all their outside activities to read.

4. The friendly cashier: There was a cashier at the Staples store in Norwalk who always said "thank you." She's the only clerk I encountered during my thirty years in Connecticut who ever acknowledged, much less looked at, me. I asked her once where she was from. She said Iowa. That explained it.

5.

6.

7.

8.

9.

10.

GOD'S WAITING ROOM

Florida haters — there are many — sometimes refer to my adopted state as "God's Waiting Room."

The haters are wrong. Everyone knows that God's waiting room, the place old people actually go to die, is Washington, D.C.

Donald Trump was inaugurated last week as America's forty-seventh president. He is seventy-eight. He replaced Joe Biden, eighty-one, who had to drop his re-election bid after claiming during a debate that he was looking forward to negotiating an end to the French and Indian War.

The month before, after she hadn't cast a vote in Congress for half a year, a reporter found Rep. Kay Granger (R-TX), eighty-one, residing in an assisted living facility in Fort Worth, suffering from dementia.

In 2023, Sen. Diane Feinstein (D-CA) died at ninety. She, too, hadn't been seen in public for months.

Left to mourn Feinstein's passing was her successor as the oldest living member of Congress, Sen. Chuck Grassley (R-IA), who is now ninety-one. He has been serving in the Senate since 1981. I was twenty-nine when he took his oath of office. I am seventy-three now.

Sen. Bernie Sanders (I-VT) is eighty-three. So is Senator Mitch McConnell (R-KY) who yesterday tumbled down the Senate steps and, when colleagues helped him to his feet, fell again.

The House of Representatives, compared to the Senate, is a preschool. A mere twenty percent of its members are seventy or older. Among them are: Bill Pascrell (D-NJ), eighty-eight; Hal Rogers (R-KY), eighty-seven; Maxine Waters (D-CA), eighty-six; Steny Hoyer (D-MD), eighty-five; and former Speaker Nancy Pelosi (D-CA), eighty-four, who has already announced plans to run for re-election in 2026. She's not going to be running in the literal sense because she broke a hip during a recent trip to Europe.

Webster's defines "elderly" as someone who is "rather old; being past middle age." Many of our elected officials aren't merely past middle age, they actually lived during the Middle Ages. Chaucer wrote about some of them in *The Canterbury Tales*.

The idea of so many elderly people leading our country should scare the shit out of all Americans, especially people my age. Though many of us like to boast we haven't lost any of the physical or mental prowess we had in our younger days, we all know that's wishful thinking. Placing politicians way past their primes into high offices — especially the presidency — is madness.

As a society, we expect dentists, brain surgeons, professional athletes and airline pilots to always, but always, perform to the best of their abilities. We should expect no less from our presidents, vice presidents and legislators, but we aren't getting it because we keep electing candidates well past their "Best If Used By" dates.

Article II of the Constitution stipulates a president has to be at least thirty-five years old. The founders clearly assumed people younger than that don't possess enough experience and/or wisdom to steer the ship of state. While I'm sure there are twenty-five-year-old *wunderkinds* who could run the country efficiently, most people that age would rather pursue a higher-paying job, like being an influencer.

The Age Discrimination in Employment Act prohibits most

employers from establishing mandatory retirement ages. Some professions, however, are exempt, including air traffic controllers, airline pilots, and public-safety workers such as police, firefighters, and correctional officers, most of whom can't work past age sixty-five. Military officers have to retire at sixty-four. Many states require judges to vacate the bench at seventy. Miners have to put down their pickaxes at sixty and racehorse jockeys have to ride off into the sunset at fifty-five.

It is time for a Constitutional amendment that requires elected Federal officials to retire once they reach a specific TBD age. Seventy seems reasonable to me. The age cap would prevent candidates within spitting distance of seventy from running in the first place.

If you worry such an amendment seems discriminatory, look at it this way: We already prevent people who aren't yet thirty-five, whose best days are presumably ahead, from serving as president. So why not prevent people twice that age, whose best days are definitely behind them? If a minimum age requirement isn't considered discrimination — it's in the Constitution after all — a maximum age requirement wouldn't be, either.

And with that, this seventy-three-year old has to wind this up because I have a lot on my plate today. Once I proofread what I just wrote, I'll take the dog on a two-mile walk, go to the gym for two more miles on the treadmill and an hour of free weights, take a bridge lesson, and go out to dinner with friends. I have plenty of energy and am firing on all eights.

Maybe I should run for senator.

MISSION IMPOSSIBLY DUMB

"Uh oh," I said to my wife when I saw the news. "The Silverspot Cinema in Naples is closing in a few days. Don't we have gift cards to that theater?"

She checked and, sure enough, we did — fifty dollars' worth. We received them years ago. We hadn't used them because there aren't many movies we want to see. Movies aren't made for people our age and/or with triple-digit IQs.

We went online to see what was playing at the Silverspot, one of those fancy multiplexes where the leather chairs recline and customers can purchase booze and food and have them delivered to their seats. Today's high-concept theaters are a far cry from the Liberty Theater in Mexico, Mo., from which I was unfairly ejected at age fourteen in 1966 because my friend Harper, who was seated next to me during *Goldfinger*, yelled, "I asked what your name was, not what you have" when James Bond (Sean Connery) asked Pussy Galore (Honor Blackman) to identify herself.

Our options yesterday were:

- *The Sound of Freedom*, a movie about child-trafficking. I keep seeing ads on social media informing me the pedophiles and Christian haters who run Hollywood don't want me to see it. Who am I to go against their wishes?

- *The Little Mermaid*, a woke remake of the Disney animated classic we took our kids to see in the early nineties. No, thank you.

- *Insidious: The Red Door*, which the review described as, "Josh Lambert heads east to drop his son, Dalton, off at school. However, Dalton's college dream soon becomes a living nightmare when the repressed demons of his past suddenly return to haunt them both." Uh, no.

- *Indiana Jones and the Dial of Destiny*, the fifth and supposedly final episode in a series of movies starring Harrison Ford as the title character. Friends were laughing about how awful it is and how ridiculous an eighty-year-old Ford — rather, his body double — looks leaping between train cars. I'd as soon have a tooth pulled as sit through that — at least I'd have the option of getting knocked out for the procedure.

- *Joy Ride*: "When Audrey's business trip to Asia goes sideways, she enlists the help of Lolo, her childhood best friend, Kat, a college friend, and Deadeye, Lolo's eccentric cousin. Their epic, no-holds-barred experience becomes a journey of bonding, friendship, belonging and wild debauchery." No wonder Hollywood is dying.

- *Elemental*, a Disney/Pixar flick described as "a modern yet fantastical odyssey of romance and self-realization clashing with the weight of ethnic and generational expectations. A colorful and cultural onslaught of imagination, relatability and sentiment, tailored by two endearing leads with irresistible chemistry." I'm not going to invest two hours of my dwindling lifespan if Disney can't explain WTF its movie is about better than that.

- *No Hard Feelings,* starring Jennifer Lawrence. I don't get Jennifer Lawrence's appeal. She was good in her first movie, *Winter's Bone,* in which she played a girl trying to track down her meth head father. Nothing she's made since is for people my age.
- *Transformers: Rise of the Beast:* Didn't bother looking up the reviews for a movie based on toys Santa brought my boys thirty-some years ago.

That left us a choice of one movie, *Mission Impossible: Dead Reckoning - Part One,* starring Tom Cruise.

The seven MI movies (to date) are based on a *Man From U.N.C.L.E* knock-off TV show from the mid-sixties about a secret agent. The original starred Peter Graves and Barbara Bain. The MI TV show is best remembered for two things: 1) Every episode began with Graves listening to a recorded message explaining what he was expected to do — his "mission" that always seemed "impossible" — which inexplicably vaporized after five seconds, and 2) its catchy theme song.

We rushed to the theater and were lucky enough to find a parking spot near the entrance, giving us just enough time to spend our gift card plus twenty dollars of our own money on two senior tickets and two gigantic tumblers of Pinot Grigio, each of which held half a bottle of wine — the bartender was filling every glass to the brim because all that booze needed to be used up before the theater shuts down for good, and he was obviously hoping for a big tip, which he duly received.

The theater was nearly full. We had to sit on the front row. Moments after we arrived, the lights dimmed and the movie began.

The opening scene: The crew of a Russian sub detects on radar something that appears to be an American sub that is about to attack.

The Russkies fire torpedoes in self-defense, and to their astonishment, the other sub disappears from the screen. Unfortunately for them, the torpedoes they fired do a one-eighty and blow their own sub to smithereens.

Cut to a Botoxed Cruise, now in his sixties, who, amazingly, has a full head of hair without a single strand of gray. He is listening to a detailed message instructing him to find a high-tech key that empowers anyone or any government who has it to create havoc then disappear, just like the sub that fired the torpedoes. The message, of course, vaporizes after five seconds. While it was possible to believe in the nineteen-sixties that Graves could remember instructions, it's totally implausible in today's attention-addled society in which nobody has the ability to remember anything unless it is entered as a reminder in their iPhones.

Cruise spends the better part of the next two hours chasing after, or fleeing from, the bad guys, and interacting strangely with two female leads who — I don't mean to sound cruel — aren't all that pretty. Whatever happened to gorgeous movie stars like Elizabeth Taylor, Julie Christie, Michelle Pfeiffer and Kim Basinger? The short answer: Kow-towing to ugly women and their supporters who claimed that glamorous women were objectionable and nothing more than sex objects, Hollywood today features interchangeable female stars of average looks and unidentifiable ethnicities.

There is no kissing, no sex, no nothing between Cruise and the females. I assume the lack of PDA is to ensure the movie will play in places like India and the Middle East, where such things can get movies banned.

From my vantage point on the front row, watching a movie in which the aging male co-stars — there are no young ones, which would make Cruise look older than he already is — are shot from below the chin to hide their sagging jowls, the most "impossible" thing about *Mission Impossible, Part 7-1*, is that none of them have a single hair protruding from their nostrils. Somehow, despite chasing each other around the world 24/7, these guys have found time to use their Wahl Nasal Hair and Eyebrow Trimmers that leave their nostrils as hair-free as a baby's behind.

Most of the movie is one action-packed scene after another, including a hot pursuit through a futuristic airport and a car chase in a yellow Fiat through Rome that passes the Colosseum and Spanish Steps. The finale takes place aboard the Orient Express as it wends its way through Austria. Predictably, Cruise chases a bad guy (or does the bad guy chase him? After half a bottle of Pinot Grigio, I wasn't sure) atop the speeding train, ducking split-seconds before the train enters tunnels. This will seem original only to anyone who has spent the last eighty years in solitary confinement — and certainly not to anyone who saw the latest *Indiana Jones* movie.

In the final scene, Cruise and one (or both, I was completely inebriated by that point) of his female stars wind up in a train dangling from a bridge that has just been blown up. The cars fall, one by one, into the abyss, and finally, Cruise parachutes to safety. The movie concludes by reminding viewers to be sure to come see *Mission Impossible, Part 7-2* which will be released in a few months.

And I will, but only if I have a gift card I have to use that day.

FOLK SONGS
FOR TODAY

I grew up listening to folk music.

My sister went away to college in 1960, when I was eight. She returned home with albums from the era's most popular folk singers including the Kingston Trio, Limeliters, Odetta, and Peter Paul & Mary, which she would play over and over until we were ordered to turn the damn stereo off.

I spent hours mooning over Mary's photo, taken in the rathskeller of some Greenwich Village club, that appeared on the cover of PP&M's first album. With her straight flowing blonde hair, I was convinced she was the most beautiful creature on earth. I mourned when she died in 2009 and like to think of her in heaven, singing protest songs to stir the angels to revolt for better conditions.

Unfortunately, most of the folk songs of the sixties make little sense to today's young folks whose hippie parents' and beatnik grandparents' embrace of the genre helped pave the way for the socially aware, hypersensitive society in which they live today. So I've taken the liberty of updating the lyrics of some of my favorites, in an attempt to add some relevance that will hopefully strike a chord (pardon the pun) with the younger generation.

Take a quick look-see at the titles on the following pages and if you don't know these songs, you can skip right over this chapter. But if you know them, I hope you'll enjoy this trip back to a kinder, more hopeful era before we all sold out.

Peace and Love.

This Land is Your Land

This land ain't your land,
This land ain't my land.
First and foremost it belongs
to native Americans from
whom we stole it which
is why we have no right
to prevent illegal immigrants
from crossing our borders today
and voting in our elections.

Blowin' in the Wind

How many roads
Must a (choose one) man/woman/trans
Walk down?
Before they call that person a
(choose one) man/woman/trans?

Tom Dooley

Hang down your head Tom Dooley,
Hang down your head and cry.
Hang down your head Tom Dooley,
Poor boy you're bound to get life
which, on appeal, will be shortened
to twenty-five years and that, thanks to our
overburdened penal system populated with
people who shouldn't be there in the first place,

means you'll be out in twelve and free
to murder more innocent young women.

The Times They Are A-Changin'

Come gather round people,
Wherever you roam.
And admit that the waters,
Around you have grown
Thanks to global warming and
Trump's rebuttal of the
Paris Climate Agreement.

500 Miles

If you miss the train I'm on,
You will know your alarm didn't go off
because you forgot to recharge your iPhone.

Puff the Magic Dragon

Puff the Magic Dragon
Lived by the sea.
And frolicked in the autumn mist
In a land called Hohnalee.
Little Jackie Paper,
Loved that rascal Puff
Which, lucky for him,
he can now buy legally
in twenty-four states
for recreational use
and in fourteen more if he can
find a doctor to claim
he needs it for a medical condition.

Where Have All The Flowers Gone

Where have all the flowers gone?
Long time passing.
Where have all the flowers gone?
Long time ago.
Where have all the flowers gone?
Gone to landfills every one where,
because they're plastic, they'll remain
for thousands of years after the young soldiers whose
graves they adorned have been forgotten.

Cruel War

The cruel war is raging,
Johnny has to fight.
I want to be with him,
From morning to night and now,
thanks to the Obama administration
which removed the military's ban on
women in combat,
I can be.

Kisses Sweeter than Wine

When I was a young man,
And never been kissed,
I got to thinking over,
What I had missed.
I got me a girl,
I kissed her and then,
Thirty years later when I was
nominated for the Supreme Court

she showed up but couldn't remember
when or where it happened.

Lemon Tree

Lemon tree, very pretty
And the lemon flower is sweet.
But the fruit of the poor lemon
Is impossible to eat
unless it is organic, free of synthetic or
artificial fertilizers and pesticides,
and grown on farms
that recycle resources while
practicing ecological balance and biodiversity.

HELP, I NEED SOMEBODY

I've been in denial for months, hoping my many issues would somehow resolve themselves but they haven't, so today I admitted defeat and called a handyman.

I hate dealing with handymen. With the exception of one excellent guy I hired years ago who disappeared and I later learned is serving a twenty-five years to life sentence, the handymen I have hired are undependable and/or inept. My theory is that every handyman who can't earn a living up north figures he might as well move to Florida where at least he can bask in his ineptitude in perpetual summer.

Another reason I hate calling handymen is that they make me feel inadequate. The reason they make me feel inadequate is because I am inadequate — clueless when it comes to fixing anything. That side of my brain not only doesn't work, it doesn't exist, so I don't know enough to stop a handyman when I see him doing something my gut tells me is wrong.

Two years ago when I called one to repair an electrical outlet in the dining room, he removed the toilet in the guest room. I assumed there was wiring under it and they were somehow interconnected. Turns out his boss had given him the wrong "to-do" list — he was supposed to remove the toilet for another client. After he reinstalled it, the toilet leaked so I had to call a plumber but he couldn't fix it. So I called another. The minute he left the kitchen faucet started leaking. For all I know, it's leaking toilet water.

So, I wait until I have a fix it list as long as my arm — and my wife insists she can't live this way another minute — before I make that call.

Right now we have, as mentioned, a leaking kitchen faucet. But that's not all. The pocket door to my wife's closet has been stuck open for at least a year, leaving a twelve-inch gap for her to squeeze through sideways. The termite guy, when he came for his annual inspection today, discovered that the pulldown door to our attic is broken so he couldn't inspect it. The house, for all I know, is being held up by termites holding hands. The French doors between the kitchen and living room have swollen from all this Florida humidity and won't shut so they need to be removed and the bottoms shaved off.

Two weeks ago the rod in one of our guest room closets collapsed, sending clothes to the floor. Last week the rod in my closet collapsed. There are burnt out can lights in our family room, bathroom and living room ceilings.

I feel like an idiot having to hire someone to replace light bulbs but the ceiling is twelve-feet high and I'm seventy-three. I'd no doubt fall off the ladder and break my hip, catch pneumonia from lying in bed unable to move, and die. I've been meaning to have the can lights in those rooms replaced with LED fixtures that supposedly won't burn out for forty-five years so I'm going to have the handyman do it. That way I won't have to get up on a ladder and change the bulbs until I'm more than a hundred years old but then, I'm sure he'll install them wrong and they'll all come crashing down. That's what happened when I had the last handyman change the fixtures in our bathroom. The new handyman can fix those, too.

A double-paned window is fogged over, the gutters are full of pine needles, the aluminum cage that towers twenty feet above our pool is covered with green slime and needs to be pressure washed, none of our exterior lights work, and the light in the swimming pool burned out after our grandson turned it off and on and off and on a hundred times. I watched a YouTube how-to video and decided I could replace it myself but got the shock of my life. Someone told me I should've turned off the circuit breaker before I started but I'm not sure what a circuit breaker is or if we even have one, so how the hell would I have known that?

The locks on all three sets of sliding glass doors are stuck and we can't open them. To get to our lanai, we have to go out the front door and circle around the house, then come in through the screen door to the pool cage. Which, come to think of it, doesn't close properly because that tube-like thingie that is supposed to make a hissing sound as it shuts is hanging off the door. Last but not least, we go on daylight savings time this weekend so the clocks in both cars need to be moved forward. Or is it backwards? I'm never sure. I always have someone do it for me.

I've asked friends for recommendations but they laugh and say they fix things around their houses themselves so no, none of them know a handyman because they, of course, have never needed one, but I'll bet dollars to doughnuts that none of those guys can conjugate Latin verbs as well as I can.

And so, once again, I have called a handyman I found online, the one whose ad has the best design and fewest typos. He said he will be here two weeks from Friday but he won't show.

They never do.

SIDE EFFECTS

Here in southwest Florida where half of all television viewers are eligible for AARP membership, TV stations rake in big bucks running commercials from pharmaceutical companies. These ads urge viewers to ask their doctors about the sponsors' products so the companies and the doctors they pay off to recommend them can rake in mega profits from you, the taxpayer, in the form of Medicare reimbursements.

Viewers are bombarded by commercials for drugs that treat low bone density, diabetes, insomnia, erectile dysfunction, toenail fungus, psoriasis, dry eyes, dry vaginas, depression, memory loss, bi-polarity, overactive bladders, thin eyelashes, low estrogen, enlarged prostates, rosacea, high cholesterol, irritable bowel syndrome, high blood pressure, weight gain, weight loss, COPD, arthritis, macular degeneration, low testosterone, and circadian rhythm disorders of the blind, among other maladies. I keep meaning to ask my doctor if any or all are right for me but then I forget. I probably need one of the memory loss drugs.

Many of the commercials feature celebrities like Cyndy Lauper promoting Cosentyx for psoriasis, and Shaq O'Neal hawking BiDill, a heart failure drug. Big pharma wants viewers to believe the celebrities are sharing information out of the goodness of their hearts because they want others to benefit from the drugs that have helped them deal with whatever disease they may be suffering from.

What the spokespeople don't reveal is how much they are being paid.

All the millions they are collecting would make anyone, even someone at death's door, feel like a teenager again. For that kind of money, these celebrities could afford body transplants and get rid of whatever afflicts them once and for all.

What annoys me most about the commercials aren't the celebrities or being reminded I live among oldsters who are already taking more drugs in one day than Janis Joplin and Jimmy Hendrix ingested during their lifetimes. It's the side effects the FDA requires the drug makers to disclose. A celeb never talks about anything unpleasant that may result from taking the drugs he or she is pimping. That task is left to an unseen announcer who cheerfully rattles off a list of side effects that would scare the shit out of anyone in their right minds as the camera follows the celebrity going about his or her upscale celebrity life.

A typical commercial goes something like this.

Celebrity *(speaking earnestly to camera)*: "Hi, I'm (imagine your favorite 40 or older celebrity here). For years I suffered from (disease or condition), but not anymore. Now I take (drug name). Just one (pill/injection/patch) and I'm good to go for up to (a time period ranging from twelve hours to six months). I don't know what I'd do without it!"
(Cut to series of quick shots of celebrity reading to children, playing croquet, dining with friends of all races, accepting a trophy and walking on a beach with a Golden Retriever as a voiceover quickly rattles off side effects.)
Voiceover: Side effects may include uncontrollable, barely controllable or somewhat controllable diarrhea, constipation, passive-aggressive behavior, depression, possession, and drooling. Do not take (drug name) with

macaroni, minestrone, pepperoni, rigatoni, communion wine or fruitcake as doing so may cause you to experience painful intercourse or vote Republican. Anyone over fifty should consult their doctor before taking (drug name) which has been known to cause side effects including sudden death, slow insidious death, ear hair, nose hair, psychosis, cirrhosis, fibrosis, trichinosis and stigmata. If you are pregnant or nursing don't take (drug name) because it's for a condition that only afflicts people who remember Elvis' first appearance on the *Ed Sullivan Show* but the FDA makes us say this.

Celebrity *(on knees in garden, holding a plant)*: "I may still have (disease or condition) but now I control it, it doesn't control me. I'm so glad I asked my doctor about (drug name). You should ask your doctor, too."

(Celebrity turns away from the camera and sticks the plant in a hole as drug logo and packaging supers over.)

BOWLED OVER

The National Collegiate Athletic Association (NCAA) today announced the addition of five new college football bowl games, bringing the total number of post-season games to six thousand ninety-two. For the first time, every U.S. college will be making an appearance in a bowl game.

According to a press release, "The NCAA board has decided that, since today's college students grew up in an era in which children received trophies simply for showing up, it makes sense to give every college football player the opportunity to say he or she has played in a bowl game. Selling the title sponsorship rights of these new games also generates revenues the NCAA can use to create awareness of college athletics and support other important endeavors."

Here are the new bowl games and the teams that will be competing in each:

Chia Pet Bowl (Jan. 11, Lifetime)
University of Northern South Dakota 0-9
University of Southern North Dakota 0-10

Master Bait & Tackle Shop Bowl (Jan 12, Discovery Channel)
Ave Maria School of Law 0-11
Sarah Lawrence 0-12

American Association of Sleep Disorders Bowl (Jan 13, Food Channel)
Alaska Bible College 0-12
San Francisco Conservatory of Music 0-11

Guadalupe's Cleaning Service Bowl (Jan. 17, ESPN II)
Texas College of Traditional Chinese Medicine 0-10
Le Cordon Bleu College of Culinary Arts (No team but will have one by kick-off)

Chair 8 at Midtown Barber Shop (Jim on Tues/Thurs/Sat; Vito on Mon/Wed/Fri; closed Sun) Bowl (Jan. 19, Golf Channel)
Wellesley 0-11
Talmudic University of Florida 0-10

PUMPING FOR INFORMATION

WELCOME
>PAY HERE WITH DEBIT CARD
> PAY HERE WITH CREDIT CARD
> PAY WITH FIRST BORN
> PAY CASHIER INSIDE

PLEASE ENTER 5-DIGIT
ZIP CODE

CHOOSE FUEL TYPE
> 93 OCTANE
> 89 OCTANE
> 87 OCTANE
> 80 PROOF

ARE YOU A MEMBER
OF OUR LOYALTY CLUB?
> YES   >NO

WOULD YOU LIKE TO JOIN?
> YES   >NO

YOU'RE SAYING
YOU DON'T WANT
FREE SHIT?
> YES   >NO

DO YOU WANT A
CAR WASH TODAY?
> YES   >NO

WHY NOT?
> WASHED IT YESTERDAY
> IT ISN'T DIRTY
> RAIN IN FORECAST
> I AM A SLOB

WOULD YOU LIKE TO
PURCHASE A
POWERBALL TICKET?
> YES   >NO

YOU CAN'T AFFORD A LOUSY
CAR WASH BUT CAN
PASS UP THE CHANCE
TO WIN A
$800 MILLION JACKPOT?
> YES   >NO

OK, SUIT YOURSELF.
COKE OR PEPSI?
> COKE   >PEPSI

METS OR YANKEES?
> METS   >YANKS

CONVICTED FELON
OR KACKLIN' KAMALA?
> CF   >KK

ARE YOUR GENITALS
THE ONES YOU
WERE BORN WITH?
> YES   >NO

THIS PUMP IS OUT OF SERVICE.

PLEASE SEE CASHIER.

DIARY OF A MAD JACK RUSSELL TERRIER

7:15 a.m. Alarm goes off. Another sunny Florida day.

7:16 a.m. Ixnay that. When dad opens the door, it's raining. He nudges me outside. I hike my leg for a split second on the bush nearest the house, then run back inside. "Good boy!" he says. Little does he know I was faking it, nothing came out. I hate getting wet.

7:24 a.m. Breakfast — one-fourth cup of Hill's Prescription Diet I/D, a tablespoon of the canned version of the same food, and two tablespoons of boiled chicken. That's all I can eat because I have irritable bowel syndrome. My dachshund brother, damn him, gets canned Little Cesar which comes in lots of flavors so at least he gets some variety in his diet. Not me. Same old, same old, meal after meal.

7:28 a.m. Pee in shower. My parents always run the water for a few minutes to warm it up before they step in it and never look down when they turn the faucet on. The water washes the pee down the drain and they are none the wiser.

7:31 a.m. The sun has come out.

8:18 a.m. Outside again to do number two.

8:24 a.m. Serial killers in giant truck appear at end of driveway. I start barking. The men steal the plastic bags dad carried out the front door last night, throw them into the back of the truck, and drive away. My barking has saved the family from certain death but do they care? Apparently not. Dad's complaining about my barking.

8:57 a.m. Mom leaves the half-empty cup of coffee she has been sipping for the last hour on an end table and goes into the other room. When she returns, she gets mad when she sees the cup on its side and me smacking my lips. How does she expect me to remain alert enough to protect this house all day without coffee?

9:34 a.m. Fall asleep atop corner cushion of family room sectional sofa. Mom's coffee must have been decaf.

10:14 a.m. Men appear on golf course behind house carrying long metal sticks. It is obvious they plan to club my family to death with those things. I growl, snarl and throw myself against the door like Cujo. They drive off in their carts, searching for victims not protected by a vicious guard dog.

10:51 to 11:34 a.m. Take walk with mom and brother but bro doesn't actually walk, he rides. Mom bought a baby carriage to wheel him up and down the street. Women stop, look inside the carriage and start talking baby talk to him as I avert my eyes. Though we look different — I'm lean, wiry and alert, he looks like a sausage — he and I share ninety-nine-point nine percent of our DNA with wolves, who are strong, brave and smart. I'm humiliated to be seen with them, they look like idiots.

12:11 p.m. Bro corners a lizard on lanai and eats it.

12:32 p.m. Man with chain saw appears in neighbor's

backyard and pretends he is there to cut a hedge. I know he's planning to use it to carve up my family. I start barking. Dad yells at me to stop, he has a headache. I can't stop, this is a matter of life and death. Twenty minutes later the man flees.

12:55 p.m. Ride with dad to CVS and stay in car as he runs inside to pick up Tylenol. En route home, dad puts the window down. I lean out and bark at people who have no business being in the neighborhood. This 'hood is crawling with escaped convicts.

1:18 p.m. Pee in front yard.

1:20 p.m. Afternoon treat — half a Hill's Science Prescription Diet I/D wafer.

2:10 p.m. Man parks van he has driven all the way from Brazil — it says Amazon on the side — in our driveway. I'm pretty sure the package he leaves on the doorstep is packed with an assortment of tarantulas, anacondas, piranhas and other deadly creatures that part of the world is known for. I run into the bedroom where dad is lying on the bed with a washcloth over his eyes — the Tylenol didn't work — and start barking to warn him. He yells at me, hurting my feelings. All I'm trying to do is keep my family safe.

2:17 p.m. Exhausted from fending off killers — mom and dad should think about moving us to a safer neighborhood — I fall asleep on sofa.

3:03 p.m. Awoken by sound of brother vomiting lizard carcass on sofa. I eat it. Mom screams.

3:05 p.m. Having consumed a warm albeit unexpected meal, I fall back asleep.

4:55 p.m. Neighbors come over for cocktails on the lanai and bring their stupid pug. I ignore the bitch as she and bro run around and around the pool until they collapse.

6:15 p.m. Dinner — same as breakfast.

6:25 p.m. Go outside and do numbers one and two.

7:02 p.m. Supervise mom and dad as they eat. Brother and I have a pact. I supervise their dinner on all days that end with "y" and promise I'll share any food that falls on the floor under the table. He is a moron.

7:30 to 8:00 p.m. Watch *Jeopardy*. It has been dumbed down since Alex Trebek's death. Every answer now contains two, sometimes three, clues. *"Known as the father of our country, America's first president is buried at Mt. Vernon."* A poodle could answer that one.

8:00 p.m-10 p.m. Curl up on sofa between mom and dad while they watch TV. (Brother is banned from it after today's unfortunate incident but they'll relent in a couple of days, they always do.) Both reach over and stroke me every few minutes. I pretend I'm asleep. "Isn't he sweet?" mom asks. "Yes, he is," dad replies. "It would be nice if he didn't bark all day, but he's otherwise perfect." Moments like this are what I live for. They make up for all the time and energy I spend protecting this family and the abuse I take for it.

10:10 p.m. Dad tries, unsuccessfully, to convince brother and me to go outside to do our business but it has started raining again.

10:45 p.m. I duck into shower for a quick pee.

11:02 p.m. Resting my head on dad's chest as he lies in bed, holding his Kindle in his left hand and petting me with his right, I vomit up what's left of the lizard carcass.

11:03 p.m. Dad turns on the shower without looking down, and lets the water run a few minutes before he gets into it.

11:41 p.m. Lights out.

GOV. NEWSOM'S GUIDE TO A COVID-FREE HOLIDAY

Dear Gov. Newsom:

I plan to comply with the precautionary guidelines you issued for Thanksgiving celebrations to prevent Californians from coming down with COVID-19. Dinner will be served outside and last two hours or less, no more than three families will attend, there will be no singing, six feet of distance will be maintained between guests, and my bathrooms will be sanitized after every use. But I have a dilemma. My four children are married and all have children of their own. Are they considered four families or are we one family?

JR in San Jose

Dear JR:

If they live with you, you are one family. If not, they comprise four separate families and don't forget that you and any other people who reside under your roof are also considered one family unit by the State of California, so we're actually talking about five families here. Tell the two children you are least thankful for that, under normal circumstances, they and their families are welcome but not this year.

Dear Gov. Newsom:

If a wildfire is raging near my home on Thanksgiving, must we still hold our celebration outside?

Frank in Fresno

Dear Frank:

Yes, but look on the bright side. You won't have to turn on the oven to roast the turkey.

Dear Gov. Newsom:

Months ago I invited eighteen guests for Thanksgiving but the balcony of my condo is only eighty square feet so it will be impossible to seat them six feet apart. What can you suggest we do?

Beverly in 90210

Dear Beverly:

Move your celebration to one of California's beautiful open spaces, like Death Valley, where there is plenty of room for you and your guests to spread out. Be sure to provide each guest with a mask and a bottle of hand sanitizer.

Dear Gov. Newsom:

I am confined to a wheelchair and unable to sanitize my bathroom between uses. If I rent a port-a-potty for my outdoor celebration, must it also be sanitized after each visit or does your edict apply only to indoor bathrooms?

Barbara in Santa Barbara

Dear Barbara:

Thanks for pointing out this critically important omission my health advisors somehow overlooked. I have extended the guidelines to require sanitizing port-a-potties and outhouses after each use.

Dear Gov. Newsom:

I'm planning a quiet Thanksgiving — just myself and my ninety-year-old aunt. We live high in the Sierras where the average temperature in late November is below freezing. Must we really a) celebrate outside and b) sit six feet apart?

Mountain Man

Dear Mountain Man:

Yes. Rules are rules.

Dear Gov. Newsom:

As a musical family, we traditionally sing our Thanksgiving prayer. We know singing isn't permissible, but would it be possible to hum it if we wear masks?

The Osmonds

Dear Osmonds:

No. Humming would violate the spirit of my guidelines. Planes equipped with listening devices will be circling our state's major cities and if they detect humming you will be subject to arrest and/or fines.

Dear Gov. Newsom:

I no longer want to live in a state in which my every move is controlled by despots like you. I am planning on jumping off the Golden Gate Bridge at noon on Thanksgiving Day. Any final advice for me?

GG in SF

Dear GG:

Make sure you stand at least six feet away from any other Californian who is doing the same thing.

A VISIT TO THE DERMATOLOGIST

I've always maintained that if you want to get rich you should study hard, become a dermatologist, and set up shop in Naples, Florida, where the sun shines brightly year-round on a sea of older folks with money and skin to burn.

As a blue-eyed old guy who never wears sun screen — I know I should, I always promise my dermatologist I will, but never do — I see mine every six months for a full body scan.

I had my regular appointment this morning. Everything checked out fine but I did have six of those brown thingies frozen off of various body parts.

The elevator I was riding to the lobby from the third floor of the clinic stopped at the second floor, and a well-dressed elderly gent wearing a straw fedora and oversized sunglasses stepped on. His skin, I noticed, was unnaturally smooth, almost translucent. Unusual for a man and a sure giveaway on a woman that she has had lots of work done on her face.

"Dr. _____" saved my life," he said, indicating the name of one of the dermatologists who works on the second floor.

"Wow," I replied. "You must have had something terrible."

"Oh no, I've never had any problems," he said. "But whenever I find a new spot, I call and she takes me in the same day."

"That's great service," I said.

"Yes. I've been here twenty eight times so far this year."

The door opened and we walked through the lobby and out into the parking lot.

He got in his Maserati convertible, waved goodbye, and drove out ahead of me.

IGUANA MIA

I couldn't imagine a more annoying neighborhood pest than the woman who, for years, has been sending vitriolic emails to residents of our development, criticizing every decision the Board of Directors makes and pooh-poohing any proposals that might cause an increase in HOA assessments. Until the day I met the four-foot Monster Iguana — I call him M.I. — who began pooh-poohing all over our house.

I first encountered M.I. last summer when our Jack Russell terrier, who was lounging by the pool, began barking hysterically and lunging at what I mistook for a palm frond that had fallen on top of the screened pool cage.

When I went outside, there was M.I. At least four feet long, he had just laid two steaming mounds of feces atop the cage. I couldn't get to him — the cage is twenty feet high and attached to the roof — so I began shouting and waving my arms. M.I. crawled leisurely off the cage, scampered onto the tiled roof, and disappeared over the side of the house. I pressure-washed the poop off the screen and backwards into the gutter. I assumed I had scared him away and that was the last I would see of him.

The following week I was reading on the lanai when I heard something shuffling overhead. M.I. was back and had just laid another horseshit-sized souvenir — just one this time, but it was at least eighteen inches long.

M.I. returned every few days for the next month, leaving another strand of shit each time. I never caught him in the act — he may have been visiting during the night — but the roof was beginning to look like a cattle feed lot. I read that iguana feces contains E. Coli and Salmonella. We spend lots of time on our lanai a few feet under its roof. So do the dogs. M.I. threatened not just our home's appearance but our health.

Iguanas aren't native to Florida, but, over the last decade, have begun popping up — make that pooping up — all over the southern part of the state. M.I.'s color was a bright lime green but iguanas can also be orange, black, pink or any combination thereof.

There's speculation some Floridian may have released a pregnant pet iguana into the wild and, ever since, they've been multiplying like, well, iguanas. Females can lay as many as seventy eggs at a time. For years they have been causing problems on the Atlantic coast but in the last few years they have moved over here to the Gulf side and have invaded communities north of us including Gasparilla Island, Cape Coral and Ft. Myers. Since Hurricane Ian in 2022, they are, suddenly, everywhere. Last week while walking the dogs, I spotted four but none nearly as large as M.I.

I asked fellow members of our community's Facebook page if anyone else in the 'hood was having problems with iguanas and, if so, what they had done to get rid of them. I didn't mention the poop — that tidbit of info was too disgusting. Nobody, it seems, was having iguana issues. Except us.

Knowing iguanas have become a problem on the golf courses in the community, I called a groundskeeper of one of the golf clubs. He put me in touch with a retired military sharpshooter who came to my house. He said he likes to use iguanas for target practice. That may sound cruel, but it's not. Iguanas can dig burrows around houses that damage foundations. Their germs can kill small animals and make humans deathly ill. They rarely attack humans but because they are an invasive species, the State of Florida forbids anyone who traps an iguana from releasing it back into the wild. It has to be destroyed.

The sharpshooter, who lives in a nearby town, said I should call him next time I saw M.I. and, if he was free, he would come right over and kill him with his pellet gun. (It is illegal to fire rifles or shotguns within the city limits so pellet guns are the only way iguanas can be shot in our town.) I showed him a video I had taken of M.I. and he said M.I. looked to be at least a twenty-pounder.

M.I. returned that afternoon — I didn't see him — and left another pile of poop. Over the next several weeks he left even more souvenirs. The three times I called the sharpshooter to grab his gun and rush over, he didn't pick up. His proposed solution, clearly, was impractical.

A friend jokingly suggested I buy a Super Soaker water gun that uses pressurized air to shoot liquids with more velocity and range than a traditional squirt gun, and fill it with vinegar — iguanas apparently hate the odor — so that, if I spotted him, I could blast M.I. through the pool screen. Made sense to me, so I bought one but was never able to use it.

As piles of poop continued to accumulate on our roof, I called a Wildlife Pest Removal Service I found online. The owner said M.I. was most likely gaining access to the roof by climbing one of the dozen trees whose branches overhang it and leaping onto it. He proposed setting a trap. He couldn't guarantee success but was almost sure the iguana would be lured into it. He said that if M.I. was trapped, he would euthanize him by placing him in a plastic bag he would put in a freezer. M.I. would gently and painlessly fall asleep. I asked if his eleven-hundred-dollar fee included a memorial service and he laughed. He said that, once M.I. was gone, he would send someone to remove the poop and treat the roof with an enzyme that would kill any germs M.I. had left behind. I agreed and the trap was set.

As if he had overheard us and wanted to express his opinion of our plan, M.I. left a jumbo-sized souvenir on the roof while I was in the driveway telling the trapper goodbye.

A few days later, a neighbor shot a huge iguana fitting M.I.'s description in his yard with his pellet gun. He said he heard the thud of the pellet penetrating the iguana's hide but, before he could reload to finish him off, the iguana crawled into a thicket of palmettos. The neighbor was almost certain the iguana was mortally wounded.

When M.I. had failed to visit the next week, I called the Removal Service and told them I didn't need the trap. M.I. was surely in iguana purgatory. The owner agreed to refund half my payment and sent a professional to remove the trap and treat the roof and pool cage with the enzyme spray.

Shortly thereafter, following several days of heavy rain that had washed the solution away, M.I. returned. More shit happened.

I finally hired a tree service to trim the branches overhanging the house from which M.I might be jumping down onto the roof. It was an all-day job that cost twenty-four hundred dollars.

We haven't seen any evidence of M.I since.

Maybe he is dead but that's doubtful. Iguanas can live up to twenty years and M.I. appeared healthy enough. Lord knows his digestive system was working perfectly. Perhaps he has given up in frustration since he can no longer access our roof. More likely, he found someone else's roof to use as his private toilet.

I hope so.

I've had it with all his shit.

TRAVELING THE WORLD
WITH A SERIAL KILLER

My wife, Judy, and I just finished the final two episodes of *Serpent* on Netflix, an eight-part mini-series about Charles Sobhrag, a French serial killer.

Sobhrag, who is serving a life term in a Nepalese prison, is believed to have murdered as many as sixteen tourists who had the misfortune to cross his path in Asia during the 1970s. Some were strangled. Some were drugged. Some he burned alive.

This is the serpentine tale of how Judy and I traveled the world thanks to Charles Sobhrag and had a swell time.

And it begins forty-one years ago, in a New York advertising agency where I was working as a writer.

Part I — 1981

Like many agency creatives, I earned money on the side as a freelancer, writing copy for companies that couldn't afford to hire big agencies but wanted advertising and marketing materials that looked like they had.

That Spring, George, an art director I worked with, told me that Royal Air Maroc, the national airline of Morocco, was looking for a writer/art director team to create an eight-page brochure about Morocco's major tourist attractions. The airline couldn't pay us in cash, but would give both of us two free first-class tickets anywhere they flew.

Judy and I had no money. We loved to travel and wanted to take a grand vacation to celebrate our upcoming thirtieth birthdays. I jumped at the opportunity.

RAM provided the photos and background materials George and I needed and we created a professional-looking guide to the country's culture and attractions.

In July, my wife and I boarded a 747 at JFK. We were off to Greece for a two-week adventure.

RAM only flew twice a week from JFK to Casablanca, and three or four times weekly from Casablanca to Athens. We would have twenty-four-hour layovers in Casablanca both coming and going. No problem. My client at RAM got us a great rate at a hotel near the center of the city, ten miles from the airport.

Following our overnight flight, a cabbie drove us over a modern four-lane highway to the hotel. That afternoon we explored the Medina, the ancient marketplace that sells everything from spices to clothes and books. The other attractions I had written about were closed for Ramadan.

The next morning we flew to Athens, where we boarded a four-day cruise on a Sad Sack of a ship — the best we could afford on our budget — bound for the Greek islands of Mykonos, Santorini and Rhodes, and Ephesus, Turkey.

Our first night at sea was rough. Almost everyone got seasick. But the rest of the cruise was blissful. Except for the leaking toilet that flooded our cabin with raw sewage.

Post-cruise we spent several days in Athens, took a tour to Corinth, and wound up our vacation at a resort where, as we relaxed on the beach, my wife read *Serpentine*, a best-seller by Tommy Thompson that recounted the horrifying story of Charles Sobhrag and his victims.

On our flight to Casablanca for our second twenty-four-hour layover, we learned our 727 had originated in Saudi Arabia. Freed from that country's laws which prohibit the sale much less the consumption of liquor, some of the Saudi passengers were ordering and drinking entire 750 ml bottles from the duty-free cart. We sat next to a Saudi who was decked out like Lawrence of Arabia, complete with headpiece and flowing robe. During the flight, he guzzled a full bottle of Johnnie Walker. Before passing out somewhere over Libya, he told us that one of the many problems he had with Americans is that we never say "shukran" — Arabic for "thank you."

The taxi line at the Casablanca airport was long. Knowing from our previous visit that few Moroccans seemed to understand English, I showed the driver a piece of paper with our hotel name on it. He nodded his head.

Several miles from the airport, the driver turned off the four-lane highway onto a dirt road where the houses were few and far between and goats were roaming.

My wife, spooked by the Sobhrag book she had just finished, grabbed my arm and squeezed hard. "Where is he taking us? This isn't the way to downtown. We shouldn't have left the highway," she whispered nervously.

I said the driver knew what he was doing; he probably made the same trip several times a day.

"No he doesn't," she said, panicking. "He's taking us out into the middle of nowhere and ... and ... *he's going to kill us!*"

The cabbie stopped the car, turned around to face us, and replied, in perfect English, "No I'm not going to kill you, this is a shortcut."

So ends Part I of my serpentine tale. Fast-forward twenty-eight years to ...

Part II, 2009

As a long-time subscriber to *Budget Travel* magazine, I had for years intended to enter the contest featured on the final page of each issue. It invited readers to submit humorous true stories of two-hundred words or less about their worldwide travels. Three or four stories were chosen for each issue. The subscriber who submitted the story deemed best that month by the editors won a trip for two to a destination provided by one of the magazine's advertisers in exchange for the free publicity.

One rainy Sunday, having nothing better to do, I wrote up the story of our trip from the Casablanca airport and the cabbie who spoke perfect English, and emailed it to the magazine.

Several months later, Judy who had just opened the mail, rushed into the room where I was sitting. "You won!" she exclaimed, waving the latest copy of *Budget Travel*. "We're going to Tasmania!"

I was thrilled. As writers often do, I had written that story for my own amusement, just to get it down on paper. The best I'd hoped for was honorable mention. Winning the grand prize was the icing on the cake.

"Where's Tasmania?" my geographically-challenged bride asked. "Somewhere in Africa?"

"It's an island south of Australia," I explained.

"Well, I hope we're flying business class. My friends who've been to Australia have all flown business class, it's too long a flight to sit in coach."

I said I doubted the flight would be in business class. It was, after all, being provided by a magazine that promoted low-cost ways to travel.

The next day I received an email from the editor confirming what I suspected. The trip consisted of roundtrip coach, not business class, flights on Qantas, Australia's national airline, from New York to Sydney. There we were to change planes and fly to Hobart, Tasmania, where we would pick up a rental car and drive around the island, staying in a different B&B for each of the six nights we were to be there.

Never having traveled down under, Judy and I agreed that, as long as we were going to be spending twenty-four hours getting there, we would at least like to see Sydney, including its renowned opera house. I said I'd contact the prize-provider, a tour company, and ask if we could lay over in Sydney at our own expense, either coming or going. I also assured Judy I had several hundred thousand American Airlines AAdvantage miles accumulated over the years, and would ask if we could use those to upgrade to business class since Qantas and American were partners in the One World frequent flyer program.

"No and no," was the response when I spoke with a representative of the tour company.

"Why?" I asked. "Because we negotiated free airfare from Qantas which can sell all the business class tickets they want to paying customers" she replied. "They don't let people flying on free coach tickets upgrade with miles. If you want to fly business class, you'll have to buy your own tickets." She said Qantas had also made it clear there were to be no layovers. That would require issuing four tickets rather than two and she wasn't willing to make them mad because she had to work closely with Qantas on a daily basis. So there.

While I didn't want to seem ungrateful for a free trip to a part of the world we had long wanted to visit, I, too, wanted to upgrade – what else was I going to do with all those miles? — and to spend time sightseeing in Sydney. Twenty-four hours from New York to Sydney was a lot of flying time just to spend six nights driving around an island between the Australian mainland and Antarctica. I called Qantas to see if we could layover and/or upgrade with miles. No, we couldn't.

When we took the trip in October, 2009, we flew business class both ways and spent our first four nights in Sydney's posh Four Seasons Hotel, overlooking the harbor and opera house. In addition to American miles, I also had hundreds of thousands of miles with Delta, which had just launched its first route between the U.S. and Australia. Delta graciously allowed me to purchase full-fare coach tickets upgradable with miles to business class. Those cost several thousand dollars each. And I paid full-price for the hotel, one of Sydney's finest. Our free trip turned out to be anything but.

We enjoyed Sydney but fell head over heels with Tasmania. It's so far off the beaten path we felt we were in a time warp. There were no malls, fast food outlets, big box stores or expressways. It was like traveling back forty or fifty years before America's small towns were destroyed by Wal-Mart and McDonald's.

Each night we stayed in a modest B&B in a different small town. One day we stopped at a seahorse museum. The next we visited a Tasmanian devil sanctuary. We toured a lavender farm. One morning we stepped out of our B&B to find our rental car surrounded by a gang of wallabies, cousins to kangaroos. We spent a day hiking around a glacial lake surrounded by snow-capped mountains.

The most memorable day of the trip was our visit to Port Arthur prison. In the early- and mid-1800s, it was England's harshest and most remote penal colony. English judges sentenced thousands of criminals to it, including children who had done nothing more than steal bread because they were hungry. Many of those prisoners, unable to afford the return passage to England, stayed on and their descendants settled Tasmania and, eventually, the mainland.

By the time our week was over, we wished we could stay longer.

Though I offered her one of the Ambien pills my doctor had prescribed to help me sleep on the seventeen-hour return flight to LAX, my wife refused. She tossed and turned in her lie-flat seat all the way across the Pacific. Once we were aboard our connecting flight to New York, she reluctantly accepted one and promptly passed out.

I had to help her stagger off the plane at JFK, deposited her in a chair while I collected our luggage, and she slept all the way to Connecticut where she was surprised the next morning to wake up in her own bed. She said the last thing she remembered was the captain announcing we were flying over Las Vegas.

And that, my friends, concludes the serpentine tale of our worldwide adventures made possible by Charles Sobhrag, the serial killer whose story you can watch on Netflix.

I hope it has inspired you to see the world but if so, please be careful and avoid any smooth-talking Frenchman who tries to befriend you. I read somewhere that Sobhrag, having served more than forty years, has applied for parole and that Nepalese authorities just may grant it.

IMPORTANT MESSAGE FROM YOUR INSURANCE COMPANY

Dear Valued Policyholder:

Tropical Storm Madison is predicted to impact the Florida peninsula as a major hurricane sometime over the next few days. As your homeowner's insurance provider, our first priority is the safety of you and your loved ones.

Accordingly, here are some tips to help you weather the storm safely:

- Keep your television tuned to a local station that features news and weather forecasts 24/7, to learn about storm shelters in your area and to find out which Home Depot stores still have plywood. If you speak English, choose a station that broadcasts in English. *Si hablas español, elige una estación que transmita en español.* IF YOU ARE HARD OF HEARING, TURN ON THE CLOSED CAPTIONS.
- Secure your property. Bring in lanai furniture, plastic flamingoes, your "Hate Has No Place Here" yard signs, and anything else that could become a projectile in high winds.
- Top off your vehicle's gasoline tank. There are only two escape routes out of the Florida peninsula — I-95 on the east coast and I-75 on the west — and both will be parking lots

packed with millions of residents trying to flee to Georgia, so it is unlikely you will be able to travel more than a few miles before you give up and return home. At least you will be able to tell your children up north, who will be calling and texting to ask where your last will and testament is hidden, that you tried to escape.

- Keep your cell phone fully charged, so you can occupy yourself during the storm taking videos of trees bending to the ground, your neighbor's roof being blown away, and storm surge that may flood your home, and sending them to your northern friends who will be posting messages on your Facebook page that they are praying for you. (Tip: Do not stand in front of picture windows to shoot videos.)

- Because you will lose power — the power always goes out on your street, even for hurricanes that hit Texas a thousand miles west of Florida — eat all the food in your freezer today. Be sure to cook meat, poultry and fish products before you consume them.

- If you have electric hurricane roll down shutters and the power goes out (which it will, see above), you will have no way to open them and will be living in complete darkness until it is restored. Remember, too, that your air conditioning system will be non-operational, so your house will be blast furnace-hot. Be sure to leave at least one window uncovered so you can break it open to allow fresh air in, and won't smother to death like a Bonita Springs couple almost did during the eleven days they were without power after Hurricane Ian.

- Stock up with water, beer, wine, Pop-Tarts, batteries and anything else you and your family will need to survive the coming days. (Note: Batteries are not intended for human consumption.) Do not assume you can count on Door Dash or Uber Eats to bring you food; they may not be operating after the hurricane since restaurants will also be without power.
- Purchase enough baby formula to last a week. If you do not have a baby, feel free to ignore this tip.
- Remember to bring any pets inside *before* the storm hits. Your policy does not cover the cost of replacing pets who blow away, drown or are eaten by alligators displaced from ponds due to the storm.

Tomorrow we will be sending you an email containing tips for surviving in what's left of your home during the weeks and months you may be waiting for checks from FEMA or us. Be advised those checks may be delayed due to the U.S. Postal Office which no longer cares about delivering anything but Amazon packages. We would like to take this opportunity to suggest you sign up today, before the power goes out and you lose your wi-fi signal, for autopay. That will allow us to deduct from your bank account any premiums you may owe now or in the future, so you won't have to worry about payments being lost in the mail.

Stay safe. Together, we will survive this storm. At least we will — this message is being sent from our headquarters in Illinois.

Remember, you're in good hands — ours and God's.

Your insurance company

10 THINGS YOUR DACHSHUND WON'T TELL YOU

1. You think we miss you when you're gone.

You desperately want to think that someone, anyone, needs and misses you when you aren't home. Sure, we yelp and wail as you're walking out the door just to mess with your head but the moment you leave, we're off to la-la land. When we're awoken by the sound of the garage door opening, we start weeping loudly, like the dogs in the YouTube videos when their masters return from overseas military duty. You assume we've been hysterical with grief the whole time.

The fact of the matter is, it's nice when you leave so we don't have to pretend we care about you 24/7.

2. How do we *really* feel about children?

Labs, Beagles, Collies and Irish Setters are said to be "good" with children. So if you, for some inexplicable reason, like human children, by all means get one of these simple-minded breeds.

We dachshunds despise children. We'll generally leave them alone, keeping a wary distance, but if they reach down to pet us we won't hesitate to bite. We know that, if push comes to shove, you'll get rid of the kids or grandkids before you'll get rid of us. We have that kind of hold over you.

3. Your home is our Poland.

Like another well-known German (OK, technically he was from Austria but this isn't a history lesson) we get off on seizing territory that doesn't belong to us and making it our own. Your favorite easy chair? Ours. Your bed? Ours. Those rooms you want to keep us out of so you can have at least a few pieces of upholstered furniture that aren't covered with stains from our incessant paw licking? Ours. Every rug in the house is ours, too. So is the driver's seat of your car. Ours, ours, ours.

4. We're little Houdinis.

We dachshunds can open any door — including locked doors — any time we want. That means you'll have no privacy, even when using the toilet. (We like to watch.) How do we do it? That's a trade secret but it has to do with applying gentle, steady pressure at the very bottom of the door, something our low stature makes it easy for us to do, which springs the latch, enabling us to waltz into rooms you want to keep us out of and open the front door when the yard men are using chainsaws to trim the shrubs and chase them away.

5. Cross us and you'll regret it.

Forbid us to enter the dining room while you're hosting a dinner party … remark to your spouse about how, just this once, you'd like to be able to roll over in bed without coming face to face with a dachshund … refer to one of us as a "wiener" (how would you like to be called, say, a "butterball?") … go on vacation and check us into a boarding kennel instead of taking us with you … and you'd better watch your back. Or, more aptly, your feet. Specifically, what they step in.

6. We're high maintenance.

Your annual veterinary bills will approximate the gross national product of Guatemala. We have extra salivary glands that generate twice the drool of ordinary dogs, so our teeth require cleaning at least twice as often. It's a long stretch between our front and rear legs so our backs can and do go out on a regular basis; a substantial percentage of us will require disk surgery costing thousands. We hate having our nails trimmed. If you try to do it yourself, we will twist and turn and shriek with so much feigned pain that you'll be afraid of injuring our backs, so you'll take us to a groomer — exactly what we wanted in the first place because we love car rides. We get bored lying around the house day after day looking cute.

7. We're one-person dogs. And that person isn't you.

For purposes of discussion, let's say there are two people in your household — Person A and Person B.

Let's assume that Person A walks us, feeds us, gives us treats when we make poo-poo or peeps outside, cleans up after us, takes us to the vet and groomer, and defends us vigorously when Person B complains about our breath and/or nonstop barking when she is trying to talk on the phone.

We will ignore Person A and lavish all our affection on Person B. Don't ask why. It's in our DNA.

8. Our favorite thing to eat is ...

something we hesitate to mention by name. But when your back is turned, we'll happily pounce on a steaming pile of this delicacy the same way you pounce on a platter of wings at a Super Bowl party. Then you pick us up and kiss us. If you only knew ...

9. We think you're an idiot.

You talk baby talk to us. You cook us beef and chicken (organic) whenever we seem bored with the expensive canned food you carefully mix with the kibble formulated to strengthen dachshund backs you special-order from Denmark. There are no repercussions when we do things that disappoint you, such as eating your sofa. (We know of one Florida couple who've had to buy one sofa for each of the seven dachshunds that have owned them during their forty-plus years of marriage. Their friends think they are idiots and so do we.)

We sleep in your bed, live in your house, lounge on your furniture, get great medical care, etc. How much do we pay? Zip. Nada. You pick up the tab for everything then allow us to rule your lives. That's as it should be. We're smarter than you and don't you forget it.

10. We're addictive.

Once you live with a dachshund, you'll never even consider another breed. Why? Re-read the last sentence of point #9.

QUICK COMEBACKS

Thanks to Boomers like me, Florida has overtaken New York as America's third-most populous state. According to demographers, a thousand people move to the Sunshine State every day. That's three-hundred sixty-five thousand new (make that "old") Floridians a year.

Florida's population will continue to grow thanks to Federal tax laws that limit deductions for property taxes and state income taxes. Both have skyrocketed in states like Illinois, Massachusetts, New Jersey and Minnesota, causing residents to flee like cockroaches when the lights come on. Van lines report they are moving three times more people to Florida than out of state.

Then, of course, there's Florida's wonderful weather. I don't have to sell you on that, it sells itself.

If you're about to retire and move to Florida, be advised that everyone — family, neighbors, friends and co-workers — will feel the need to express their opinions. Some will say they're happy for you. Some will say they are jealous and can't wait to make the move themselves. And others — perhaps the majority of folks around your own age — will make comments so ignorant and/or nasty you'll have trouble refraining from decking them.

Why? Because you are their contemporary. The fact that you are retiring to Florida makes them feel old, a state of being many

Boomers refuse to acknowledge. If *you* are old enough to move to Florida, then *they* must be old enough to move, too. That, for some reason, makes them feel compelled to explain why they would never consider it.

Here, for your convenience, are quick comebacks to some of the most common comments you will hear when you tell people you're moving to Florida.

"I went to Florida once and hated it — it's so phony."

"You took your family to *Disney World* for Chrissakes. Disney World isn't *real.*"

"Why would I move to Florida? My children and grandchildren live here."

"In case you haven't noticed, your children haven't lived with you for twenty years. And your grandkids don't even look up from their video games to acknowledge you when you visit. How often do you see them anyway? When was the last time I saw one of their cars in your driveway? Thanksgiving? Christmas? Have you ever considered they might actually *want* to come see you and spend the holidays on a Florida beach rather than driving through a blizzard to your current house that smells musty because you haven't been able to open the windows since October?"

"I'd miss the four seasons."

"You would miss raking leaves, picking up fallen branches after sleet storms, shoveling show and paying fuel oil bills that, in any given month between November and April, amount to more than you made in a year on your first job?"

"There's no culture in Florida."

"Au contraire." (Be sure to use that term. It's French, which means you know a thing or two about culture.) "There's the Tampa Bay Buccaneers, Miami Heat, Jacksonville Jaguars, two ACC and one SEC college football teams, the Daytona 500, the Don Garlits Museum of Drag Racing, the Live Mermaid Theater in Weeki Wachi Springs and Dolly Parton's Dixie Stampede in Orlando. What more could you want?"

"I can't stand Southerners."

"So don't move to Mississippi. Everyone in Florida is from the north. People who live in other southern states already enjoy mild winters so they don't move there."

"What will you do all day?"

"Whatever I want to do. I can golf, play tennis or pickleball, go to the beach, sail, take walks, ride my bike, make new friends who don't talk about their children or grandchildren all the time and are always free to play cards or mah-jongg or go to happy hour or dinner. What will you be doing when the snow's so high you can't open your front door?"

"What if you hate it?"

"I'll move back. At least I am willing to try something new rather than ramble around a house that's too big for my needs that I have to spend most of my disposable income to maintain while growing old in a town geared to young families with no social services whatsoever for its senior citizens."

"Florida's too flat."

"You really are desperate, aren't you?"

"It must be a million degrees in summer,"

"Yes, northern and central Florida — Tallahassee, Pensacola, Jacksonville, Orlando and The Villages, for instance — experience hot, humid summers. But the southern half of the state, the part below the frost line which runs roughly from Sarasota to Vero Beach, enjoys tropical weather that doesn't vary all that much from month to month. Temperatures rarely reach the mid-nineties, even on the Fourth of July. The highest temperature ever recorded in Naples and Ft. Lauderdale was ninety-nine degrees. Miami reached one hundred exactly once, on July 21, 1942. How many one hundred-plus degree days will you have to endure summer after summer? Your northern A/C bill will be higher in summer months than mine.

"Will you ever be back?"

"Yes, for your memorial service unless you die during the winter in which case I'll send a spray of flowers and raise a glass to you at the country club bar.

SHORTS STORY

I am confident I'm speaking for the majority of my gender when I say I hate shopping for clothes. Women shop for clothes (and accessories and make-up and jewelry) as a form of recreation. Men shop only when they have to.

Have you ever met a man who, when you asked what he did that day, replied, "I went to the mall, tried on clothes, bought several bags full, brought them home, tried them on again, then decided I didn't like them, so I plan to take them back and get my money refunded so I can do it all over again?" Of course not.

Happily, my wife loves to shop so she buys all my shirts, underwear and socks. Being retired and living in the tropics, I have little need to buy slacks or, as I call them, long pants. I do, however, have to shop for shorts, which I wear three hundred-sixty-five days a year.

For months my wife, who does the laundry — she forbids me from going anywhere near the washing machine, she says I don't understand fabric — has been complaining that all my shorts are frayed or stained. She says she is embarrassed to be seen with me. This morning I reluctantly agreed to go to the mall to buy some new ones. I'm a weird size so I generally have to spend at least half a day going from store to store, rummaging through racks and shelves full of shorts in every size but mine, hoping to find at least a couple of pairs that fit so she'll get off my back.

I got lucky today. At Dillard's, the first store I visited, a helpful salesman pulled off the shelf a pair of size thirty-three shorts from a shipment he said had arrived overnight. When I tried them on, they fit perfectly — as perfectly as shorts can fit on a man who has no discernible butt. (I've lost my ass twice — during the 2008 financial crisis and again at some point over the last ten years). I bought six pairs in different colors.

I was home a half hour after I left – and that's including the twenty minutes it took to drive to and from the mall. My wife was incredulous.

"Why didn't you look at other stores?" she asked.

"Because these fit."

"But how do you know they fit? You couldn't have possibly tried them all on."

"I tried on one pair. It fit, so the others will, too."

"How can you be sure you wouldn't have found some you like even better somewhere else?"

"These fit. They are fine."

"But they are all just alike except for the color."

"What's your point?"

"You don't get shopping," she said.

Perhaps I don't get shopping any more than I understand fabric.

All I know that is that, mercifully, I won't have to do it again for another year.

NURSERY RHYMES FOR THE 21ST CENTURY

Rock a Bye Baby

Rock a bye baby,

In the treetop.

When the wind blows,

The cradle will rock.

When the bough breaks,

The cradle will fall.

Then we'll sue the tree service

For not telling us this could happen.

Jack and Jill

Jack and Jill went up the hill,

To fetch a pail of water.

Now they live in foster homes

Because Social Services says children

need to live in buildings with running water.

Round the Mulberry Bush

Round and round the mulberry bush
The monkey chased the weasel.
The monkey thought t'was all in fun
Until the weasel demanded a safe space
and that the zookeeper resign for failing to provide one.

This old man

This old man,
He played one.
He played knick-knack on what I had always told myself
was my thumb but, with the help of my therapist,
have come to realize was a part of me nobody should ever,
ever touch without asking which is why I'm coming forward
after all these years.

Pat-a-cake, pat-a-cake

Pat-a-cake, pat-a-cake,
Baker's man.
Bake me a gluten-free, dairy-free, nut-free cake
As fast as you can.

The old woman in the shoe

There was an old woman who lived in a shoe,
She had so many children,
She didn't know what to do
Thanks to Republicans who blocked funding
for Planned Parenthood.

Old MacDonald

Old MacDonald
Had a farm
E-I-E-I-O.
And on his farm he had some chicks
But they weren't free range so PETA picketed the nation's
leading supermarket and restaurant chains urging them
not to sell Farmer McDonald's eggs
 so now he's a greeter at Walmart.

Georgie Porgie

Georgie Porgie, pudding and pie.
Kissed the girls and made them cry.
Now he's on the list of registered sex offenders.

Little Tommy Tucker

Little Tommy Tucker
Sings for his supper.
What shall we give him?
White bread and butter.
How can he cut it
Without a knife?
How will he be married
Without a wife
Or husband?

WHITE LEG SYNDROME

Women are always complaining about the physical changes they undergo as they get older. We men don't go around talking about the changes we experience as we age but they trouble us nevertheless.

Our hairlines recede and sometimes disappear altogether. The only new hairs we see are the ones that inexplicably sprout from our noses, ears or eyebrows. It starts taking a long time to pee. Our blood pressure shoots up. Many require pills to achieve something they used to try to disguise whenever it popped up inappropriately at work, church or during a PTA meeting. But of the many afflictions aging males face, the one that troubles me most is one nobody talks about: white leg syndrome.

I'm outside under Florida's blazing sun for hours each day. I walk the dog two or three miles, read or write by the pool and occasionally, even work in the yard. My every waking moment is spent wearing shorts or swim trunks.

Though I promise my dermatologist I'll wear sunscreen, I never do. As a result, my face is perpetually tan. So are my arms. But my legs, which receive every bit as much exposure to the sun, are the color of Styrofoam.

I first noticed this phenomenon as I was working out in front of a mirror at the gym. I thought it was a giant sunspot reflecting off the mirror but no – those were my legs shining back at me. Looking around,

I observed that the legs of roughly half the men my age were as tan as their faces. The other half had legs as pale as mine.

I asked my wife if she had noticed how white my legs had become. "Duh, you're just now noticing that?" she replied. "They look…bizarre."

On my next visit to the dermo, I asked, "Do some men lose melanin in their legs as they get older?" He laughed. "That's ridiculous. Your legs are white because your upper body is casting a shadow that blocks the sun from reaching them." I might buy that explanation if I were the size of Illinois Governor Pritzker, but I'm not.

I don't want to sound vain and/or vapid here. I realize there are many men my age or older who would gladly trade their very real physical maladies for one as insignificant as mine. I suppose I could go to one of those spray-tanning places or slather a mixture of baby oil and iodine onto my legs, as my sister used to do to her entire body when she was a teen, to attract the sun's rays. I could even hide my lily whites with knee-high socks and try to pass myself off as a Bermudian. But none of those alternatives are acceptable.

Clearly, white legs are something I will have to live with. Unlike the hair that sprouted from my left ear while I was sleeping last night that, this afternoon, is approximately the length of a bamboo fishing pole.

I'm going into the bathroom to tweeze that sucker right now.

A TERRIFYING TRIP DOWN MEMORY LANE IN A WHITE FORD GRANADA

"Wow, look at that!" I exclaim as we pull into the left lane of the interstate to pass a white 1976 Ford Granada with a padded vinyl roof, whitewall tires and a blue Florida license plate stamped "antique."

"Look at what?" my wife asks.

"We had one just like it."

"When?"

"In Chicago."

"I don't remember a car like that. What kind is it?"

"A Ford Granada. You drove it every day for two years. You would drop me off at work then continue on to your job."

"No I didn't."

"We bought it from a dealer in Evanston after we found out it was going to cost a hundred bucks every month to park both our cars in the garage of our condo. We traded in your old blue Plymouth Belvedere and my yellow Mustang you couldn't drive because it was a stick shift to save on parking fees."

"What kind of car did you say it was?"

"A Ford Granada. First car we ever had with an FM radio. It had a 302 V-8 and a green interior. We sold it to an art director I worked with a couple of days before we moved to New York."

"You're making this up."

"Why would I make something like that up? You're getting senile. You scare me."

"Remember when we went to Granada?"

"No. What are you talking about?"

"On that trip to Spain the summer we moved to New York."

"We didn't go to Granada. We went to Malaga and Marbella but we most definitely didn't go to Granada."

"Yes we did. One day we decided we had spent too much time on the beach so we drove to Granada to see the Alhambra."

"No we didn't."

"Granada is up in the mountains. The road was twisty. I was terrified. You were going too fast. You always do. Slow down."

"You're out of your mind."

"We toured the castle. It was built by the Moors. Then we walked the grounds. They were beautiful. We bought a copy of *The Alhambra* in the gift shop."

"James Fenimore Cooper?"

"Washington Irving. It's in the bookcase in the den. I'll show you when we get home."

"No you won't because you're delusional, it's not there."

"You're the one who's delusional. If we'd had a car like that, which we didn't, I'd remember it. You're scaring me. How could you forget the Alhambra? It was magnificent."

"If we had actually been to Granada, I'd remember it."

When we arrive home she pulls a book from the shelf and hands it to me triumphantly.

"Here you go, *The Alhambra* by Washington Irving. Printed in Spain in 1978, the year we moved to New York. Why would we have this if we hadn't bought it in Granada?"

I go into a guest room, rummage through a chest of drawers, and emerge ten minutes later with an album containing a faded photo of her wearing a blue down jacket and stocking cap, standing next to a white Ford Granada with a padded roof.

"Who did you say you are again?" she asks.

We laugh. But not too hard.

INTERVIEW TIPS FOR NEW COLLEGE GRADS

The Wall Street Journal reports that some newly-minted college graduates are demonstrating what potential employers describe as "bizarre" behavior during job interviews. Human resource professionals say that one in five now exhibit what they refer to as "quirks."

One recruiter complained about an applicant who brought a caged cat she played with throughout the interview. Another expressed annoyance about candidates who take calls and send text messages. One described an applicant who brought his father along to the interview, then took further offense when dad called to negotiate his son's salary. (Personally, I think it showed gumption on the kid's part to recognize that his dad had more experience in that department.)

Apparently, it's getting tougher and tougher for kids to land their first post-college jobs, even in today's robust economy.

Over the course of my career, I interviewed hundreds of job applicants, many of them fresh out of college. Some were understandably nervous, and I always tried to put myself in their place, remembering how I felt when I was their age. (Sidebar story: Once, when I was interviewing a candidate to work on our CBS-TV account, I asked what shows he watched. He replied, "I refuse to watch TV, it's stupid." He did not get the job.)

Here's a helpful list of interview tips new grads can follow to ensure they make good first impressions and land the job of their dreams.

Earbuds: It's fine to wear them in the waiting room – you don't want to have to talk to some chatty receptionist if you arrive early – but be sure to remove them and stash them in your pocket before you go in to meet with the interviewer.

If the interviewer asks if you would like something to drink: It's OK to request a bottle of water or, if you were up all night, can of Red Bull. It's not OK to request a tall half-skinny half two-percent extra hot split quad shot – two shots regular, two shots decaf – latte with whip, unless you know for sure there's a Starbucks in the lobby and you noticed the interviewer's assistant didn't seem to be all that busy.

Drug tests: If the subject comes up, it's not considered good form to ask, "Do I really have to take one?" If the interviewer says all applicants must pass such a test, don't request that it be scheduled for a month after your start date.

Tattoos: Ink on your arms, neck and/or face shows you're a conformist like everyone else and that's exactly what big companies want so by all means display yours with pride and consider getting more.

Do not bring: Your parent(s). It's fine to bring your gf, bf, bff, dog, cat, snake, gerbil, ferret or hamster as long as s/he is well behaved.

Do bring: Your resume. And make sure it's on paper (a material made from wood. Ask your grandparents).

Dress for success: Be sure to wear a top and bottom of some sort. If you wear a hoodie or stocking cap, remove it for the interview. Females and male-to-female transgendered applicants have the option, if they wish, of wearing a dress.

Demonstrate interest in the company: It's important to give the illusion you are interested in the company, its mission and policies. One way to do that is to, at the end of the interview when you are asked if you have any questions, actually ask some. If you can't think of any, here are some you might want to consider.

- When I'm working from home, can I use the company credit card to order lunch?
- Where is the holiday party held and how many friends can I invite?
- How long until I get a company-paid car?
- Does your insurance cover my pets?
- When I travel, do I get first class or do I have to sit in business class?
- Does your cafeteria serve Coke or Pepsi products?
- What, exactly, do you people do?

Follow these tips and you'll have a job quicker than you can say, "Dude, I'm stuck in an interview. Call back in a few."

I HOPE YOU (WON'T) DANCE

I'm a lousy dancer. I have no rhythm. Most white men don't.

Years ago my wife, a good dancer, signed us up for ballroom lessons. After a couple of weeks the instructor took us aside and asked us — he was looking at me — to drop out. He said he was having to spend so much time correcting my technique that I was holding the class back. My wife was embarrassed and disgusted.

On a trip to Argentina — she should have known better — she insisted we take tango lessons. Same thing happened. (For the record, "No! No! No!" in Spanish is screamed the same way it is in English.)

Though I can't dance ballroom style, I have always been able to flap my arms and shuffle my feet whenever we're attending a function where a band or DJ is playing classic rock. But I'm not going to do that anymore either.

Our friends Tim and Jeane recently invited us to join them for the Tree-mendous Tuesday buffet at their country club here in Florida. Tim and Jeane are our age. Most members of their club are too, and some are even older. A seventy-ish long-haired man with a karaoke machine was singing songs from the fifties and sixties. The dance floor was packed with Boomers. My wife, I could tell from the way she was bouncing around in her seat, wanted to dance, so I stood up and took her hand to lead her out to the floor.

"Are you guys coming?" I asked Tim.

"God no," he said, indicating the dance floor filled with people flailing about to *Mony Mony*. "Old people fast-dancing. It's the *ugliest* thing I ever saw."

In that moment of clarity I realized ... *he's right*.

There's nothing wrong with Medicare recipients slow-dancing to *Unchained Melody* or *When A Man Loves a Woman*. It's sweet to see a couple with decades of shared history holding each other close, wondering if that's a song they danced to at their prom or wedding.

But old people convulsing to *Heat Wave, Expressway to Your Heart* or other frenetic oldies look ridiculous. Especially when it's obvious they're not enjoying themselves and are just doing it to prove they still have some fire in their bellies.

My idea of hell is being sentenced to watch for eternity what I was forced to witness at a restaurant the other night: a dance floor filled with senior citizens mechanically and joylessly doing the swing to *Teenager in Love*.

> *Each time we have a quarrel,*
> *It almost breaks my heart.*
> *Cause I'm so afraid,*
> *That we will have to part.*
> *Each night I ask the stars up above.*
> *Why must I be a teenager in love?*

Why, indeed? I moved to the other side of the table so I wouldn't have to watch.

There are lots of ways those of us who remember watching *American Bandstand* on a black and white TV can shake our collective booty. We can bike, jog, hike, take walks, pump iron, do yoga, and ski. We can roller blade, swim laps, take aerobic classes, snorkel, surf, kayak, windsurf and play tennis, golf, volleyball, badminton, croquet or bocce. We can sky-dive, para-sail or climb mountains. Those with rhythm, grace and/or style can take up ballroom dancing and glide around like the folks on *Dancing with the Stars*.

But fast-dancing?

Do yourself and everyone around you a favor: Don't.

CAR SALESMAN

Car salesman (*to me, as I am looking inside an SUV parked on the showroom floor*): Beautiful, isn't it?

TD: It is, but I'm actually interested in a sedan. An S-Sixty specifically. I don't see one here on the floor. Do you have any outside on the lot?

Salesman: I don't know. I'm new here, I'm not allowed to sell cars yet, only to show them.

TD: That's why I'm here today — to see an S-Sixty. I've read the reviews and they sound great.

Salesman: I'll go to the back room and get the keys to one.

TD: Sounds good.

Salesman (*returning five minutes later*): Uh, my boss said we don't have any V-Sixties.

TD: I didn't say V-Sixty, I said S-Sixty. The V-Sixty is a station wagon. An S-Sixty is a sedan.

Salesman: Sorry, I'm still learning the differences between the models. It's confusing. I'll get the keys.

TD: I'll wait.

Salesman: *(10 minutes later):* I found the key to a blue one with tan interior. It's parked outside.

TD: Great, that's the combination I'd want. Let's go see it.

Salesman *(three minutes later, pressing the key fob and opening the door to a blue SUV)*: Here we go, an EX-Sixty.

TD: I want to see an S-Sixty. A s*edan*, not an SUV.

Salesman: Oh. I guess I just heard the Sixty, not the S. I'll go back and get the key to one.

TD *(pointing to a car across the lot)*: Isn't that an S-Sixty?

Salesman: If you say so.

TD: It is.

Salesman: Give me a minute, I'll be right back.

TD: OK.

(Salesman goes back in the showroom and emerges five minutes later, looking sheepish.)

Salesman: Uh, this one's a demo. Boss says we aren't able to sell it.

TD: All I want is to look inside — to sit behind the driver's seat and get a feel for it. Can't I at least I sit in that one?

Salesman: Oh. OK. In that case, I'll get the key. Can I grab you a bottle of water while I'm inside? This dealership has bottles with their own label.

TD: No thanks.

Salesman: You sure I can't get you one? It's hot out here.

TD: No, I just want to see the inside of an S-Sixty. That's S as in Sam, six, zero.

(Salesman returns ten minutes later.)

Salesman: I'm sorry, but this one's sold, someone's coming to pick it up tomorrow.

TD: That's fine, but did you get the key?

Salesman: Uh, no. When the boss said it was sold, I ...

TD: I have to go. Thanks for your time.

Salesman: No, don't leave. I'll run back and get the key. Gimme a minute.

TD: OK.

(Five minutes later.)

Salesman: Here we go. *(Pressing the key fob and opening the door.)* So, what do you think?

TD: I don't know yet. Let me sit behind the wheel.

Salesman: These are the safest cars in the world.

TD: I know, I've owned three.

Salesman: Only one person has ever been killed driving one and that's because he wasn't wearing his seat belt.

TD *(sliding behind the steering wheel):* I can't believe that. Of the millions of these cars that've been sold around the world in the last fifty years, only one person has ever died in an accident?

Salesman: That's what someone said.

TD: Seems far-fetched.

Salesman: What do you think?

TD: The leather's beautiful. This is real leather, right? And I love this dashboard, it's one big computer that reminds me of a jet cockpit. Are you *sure* you don't have another S-Sixty in that lot off to the side over there? I see dozens of cars. At least one of them has to be an S-Sixty I could take for a test drive, no?

Salesman: Now you want to go for a test drive? I thought you just wanted to look inside.

TD: I did. And because I like what I'm seeing, I'd really like to drive one if you have one available. Not far, maybe a mile or two. Just to see how it handles.

Salesman: So, if you're buying one today. I'll have to get my manager for that. I can't sell, just show.

TD: I didn't say I was buying one today. But I don't think it's too much to ask to see the inside of a car and take it for a test drive before I decide whether to buy it.

Salesman: Let me get the manager and see if we can work out a deal.

TD: Never mind. I'm leaving now, but before I go, let me ask you something. Is this the first job you've had selling cars?

Salesman: Yes.

TD: How long have you been here?

Salesman: This is my second week.

TD: What'd you do before that?

Salesman: Waiter.

TD: For how long?

Salesman: A few months. I hated it. People are so rude.

TD: And before that?

Salesman: I worked at Macy's.

TD: Doing what?

Salesman: Selling menswear. I bought this shirt and tie with my employee discount. Do you like it?

TD: Very nice. How long did you work at Macy's?

Salesman: Eight days. Wasn't for me. I got my degree last year. I don't want to sell clothes for a living.

TD: What was your major?

Salesman: Business. I'm going for my MBA at night.

TD: I'm taking off.

Salesman: Can I have your contact information?

TD: Give me your card and if I decide to move forward, I'll be in touch.

Salesman: They're still at the printer.

TD: What's your name?

Salesman: Paul. Hope you'll remember it.

TD: Well, Paul, I won't be forgetting you.

Salesman: Be sure to ask for me when you come back. I don't have a desk yet so I'll probably be back in the employee lounge.

TD: OK, Paul. I will. Bye.

DRYDEN'S LAWS

Murphy only had one law. I have more. Many more. Here goes:

- The sun will be shining when your car enters the car wash. Two minutes later, when it emerges, the sky will have turned gray. It will rain on the way home. The sun will come out as you turn into your driveway.
- When you're in a hurry and have chosen the express check-out line, the cashier's receipt printer will jam or run out of paper and she will have to call her supervisor over to fix it.
- When you finally find an article of clothing or pair of shoes you like, the store will have it in every size but yours.
- The door prize will go to the person who entered just ahead of you.
- As you are stepping onto the plane, the flight attendant will announce the overhead bins are full so your carry-on has to be checked.
- On those rare occasions you actually need cash, your bank's ATM will be out of service and the screen will direct you to a branch five miles away where the ATM works. When you get there, that ATM will be out of service and the screen will direct you back to the one you originally visited.

- When you see a story you want to read online and click on the headline, it will turn out to be a video.
- Every time you are sure you've overpaid your taxes, you have underpaid. When you are sure you've underpaid, you've overpaid.
- The kitchen will be out of whatever you ordered but your waiter won't tell you that until he has served everyone else in your party.
- After you've waited in a phone queue for hours, listening to recorded messages telling you how important your call is, the person who finally picks up will cut you off.
- When you travel a thousand miles to a wedding, looking forward to reconnecting with friends and family members you haven't seen in years, the loud music at the reception will make it impossible for you to talk with them.
- The ice maker of your new refrigerator, which cost more than your first house, will spring a leak while you are traveling and you will return to find your house flooded, floors ruined, and mushrooms growing from the ceiling.
- When you spring for first-class, your nonstop flight will be canceled at the boarding gate and you'll be placed on the next available flight that leaves at 5 a.m. tomorrow. You'll be assigned a middle seat of the last row in coach, which doesn't recline, and will be required to connect in Charlotte or Atlanta.
- In the middle of a renovation project, after the demolition but before your new cabinets, sinks, faucets, countertops, flooring, etc. have been delivered, your contractor (whose recommendations were impeccable, all your friends used him) will:

A) announce he has just been diagnosed with a terminal illness that may prevent him from finishing the job

B) declare bankruptcy after you've advanced him money to buy materials he hasn't yet delivered

C) claim he is unable to give you a completion date because his helpers have been deported

D) all the above if your last name is Dryden

HAPPY BAY ACTIVITIES NEWSLETTER

Here, to help you plan your social calendar, is a partial list of upcoming activities available to you, as a resident of Happy Bay Golf & Beach Club, Florida's friendliest community. Register at least two days in advance for the events you wish to attend and be sure to visit our website for the full list.

Go with the flow: Gentlemen, do you have to get up three or four times at night to go to the bathroom? And once you get there, do you stand over the toilet, waiting for something to happen while you try to conjure up images of Niagara Falls? If so, plan on attending an informative seminar, "Prostate With(out) Grief," presented by Jerry Tull MD, who will be explaining the Uro-Lift, a minimally invasive procedure that lifts swollen prostate tissue out of the way of the urethra. It will be held on Tuesday, April 6 at 11 a.m., followed by cocktails and lunch.

There's a Ford in your future: Happy Bay resident Patti Horton, winner of the Scranton Thespian Society's coveted "Best Actress" award in 1982, will be appearing in her acclaimed one-woman show, "The Wit & Wisdom of Betty Ford," at 1:30 p.m. on Wednesday, April 7. Tickets are $20 and include cocktails before, during and after the performance.

Woodstock Revisited: If you weren't able to attend the real Woodstock, here's your chance to make up for it Thursday, April 8 at 5 p.m. at the beach pavilion. Members of the Happy Bay Chorale will be re-creating many of that legendary event's most memorable moments including performances of *Joe Hill* by Joan (Marilyn Rosenthal) Baez, *Purple Haze* by Jimi (Dr. Stephen Bing) Hendrix, *Piece of My Heart* by Janis (Charlotte Hoffman) Joplin and *With A Little Help From My Friends* by Joe (Gregory Williams) Cocker. Cocktails will be available from the outdoor bar until the event's conclusion at 7:30 p.m. Be there or be square!

9-hole ladies: Will be holding their monthly scramble beginning at 9 a.m. sharp Saturday April 10 at the golf club. The ladies will be playing the Panther course this year. Beverage service will be available at holes 2, 4, 6 and 8.

Book signing: Resident Roger M. Oswald has released his long-awaited memoir, "Growing Up Oswald," his sometimes poignant and at times hilarious account of coming of age in the 1960s as Lee Harvey Oswald's fourth cousin twice removed. A reading, book signing and cocktail reception will be held on Monday April 12 at 7 p.m., at the Community Center. Proceeds from the sale of books will be donated to the NRA.

Cocktail fundraiser: Will be held Sunday, April 18, from 4 p.m. until ??? at the Tennis Center to raise funds for the next cocktail fundraiser currently scheduled for Sunday, May 4. $20.

Tequila Sunrise sail: The HMS Pelican departs every Wednesday at 6 a.m. from the marina for a three-hour cruise through our beautiful bay during which you can observe the sunrise and partake of Captain Meacham's famous "liquid breakfast" for just $4.50/glass.

Shirley Johnson Memorial Service: Services will be held in the Grill Room on Saturday, April 24 at 2 p.m. for longtime resident Shirley Johnson who succumbed to injuries suffered during a Kayak Club outing last month. While our community is blessed with a profusion of beautiful lakes and abundant wildlife, Shirley's family has asked us to take this opportunity to once again remind all residents and guests not to feed the alligators. A cocktail reception will take place immediately following the service.

YOU, TOO, CAN BECOME A PUBLISHED AUTHOR

I recently ran across an article entitled, *Five Things to Do to Get Your Book Published*. It listed — as you might expect — five steps for aspiring authors. Here they are, in order:

> **1. Come up with an idea for your book.** "Having an original or inspired idea is always useful..."
>
> **2. Decide *who* you are writing for.** Are you writing a book for children? If so, write using language they can understand. If your book is for adults, consider using bigger words. (The writer didn't suggest that if, say, you are writing for a Japanese audience, you should write in the Japanese language rather than Albanian, Hebrew, English, etc. but that might be a good idea, too.)
>
> **3. Finish your manuscript.** "Create a schedule and write regularly" until your manuscript is complete.
>
> **4. Consider hiring an agent.** An agent can help sell your manuscript, a key step to becoming a published author.
>
> **5. Keep your options open.** Approach large, medium and small publishing houses to see if they will pay you for the privilege of publishing your book. If none of the large, medium or small publishers express interest, maybe you can pay one of them to print it for you.

I was so taken by the brilliance of the advice that I read the article twice. I always wondered why none of my books had been published. It never occurred to me that I have been overlooking steps 1, 2 and 3 all these years.

Now that I'm completing this, the final chapter of my book, I've realized these five steps just begin to "scratch the surface" of the many things aspiring authors must do. So I have spent the last two weeks interviewing fellow authors to develop five more tips to share with my readers in case you, too, have been wondering how to get your book published.

6. Use words and/or pictures to make your book "come to life." Each and every author I interviewed was emphatic about this: *Readers prefer books with something other than blank pages.* One noteworthy exception: A book entitled *The Achievements of Kamala Harris* containing one hundred ninety-one pages of nothingness, was an Amazon best-seller in the fall of 2024, earning hundreds of five-star reviews. Kudos to my fellow author, Jason Dudash.

7. Give your book a title. A "catchy" one will do wonders to attract attention to your book. If you have trouble coming up with one, consider variations of titles other best-selling authors have used with success. For instance, *Gone with the Breeze, A Tale of Two Suburbs, To Kill an Oriole, The House of the Seven Bathrooms* or *The Catcher in the Pumpernickel.*

8. Submit your manuscript on paper or digitally to potential agents and publishers. Unless you are a former president, first lady, Kardashian or other celebrity, it is unlikely publishers will agree to print your book much less send you a large cash advance if they aren't able to read it before it goes to press.

9. Play the "name game." I don't mean the 1960s song by

Shirley (*Shirley Shirley Bo Berly Banana Fanna Fo Ferley, Fee Fie Mo Merley*) Ellis. I'm talking about something more important that is absolutely crucial to your success. When you send your manuscript to an agent or publisher, be sure to put your *name* and *contact information* on the title page and on the cover letter you enclose.

10. Breathe, eat, sleep and eliminate waste during the time you are writing your book. That will enable you to complete the other nine critical steps.

Follow these steps and it's a "sure thing" you will have a successful career as a best-selling author. If you become discouraged, re-read them and tell yourself: "If that idiot Tom Dryden can write a book, I can, too!"

Thanks for reading *Retired & Moved to Florida.*

ABOUT THE AUTHOR

An advertising writer for thirty-five years, Tom Dryden is a husband, father and grandfather. He retired and moved to southwest Florida with his wife and two spoiled dogs.